Benjamin Ward Richardson

The Son of a Star - A Romance of the Second Century

Vol. I

Benjamin Ward Richardson

The Son of a Star - A Romance of the Second Century
Vol. I

ISBN/EAN: 9783744776417

Printed in Europe, USA, Canada, Australia, Japan

Cover: Foto ©Thomas Meinert / pixelio.de

More available books at **www.hansebooks.com**

THE

SON OF A STAR

A ROMANCE OF THE SECOND CENTURY

BY

BENJAMIN WARD RICHARDSON

IN THREE VOLUMES

VOL. I.

'*Ficta voluptatis causâ sit proxima veris*'—Hor.

LONDON

LONGMANS, GREEN, AND CO.

AND NEW YORK : 15 EAST 16th STREET

1888

TO

MY WIFE

MARY J. RICHARDSON

I DEDICATE

WITH ALL MY HEART

THIS BOOK

'THE SON OF A STAR

LONDON
25 MANCHESTER SQUARE
Midsummer Day 1888

CONTENTS

OF

THE FIRST VOLUME.

THE SON OF A STAR.

CHAPTER I.

AN OPENING VISION.

COME, my reader, come, and for a few short hours dream with me. We shall not waste time in a dream, since dreams, however intense, are, usually, the fleeting passages of our idle hours. For all that we may, perchance, realise much that partakes of action, make many new acquaintances, and learn the details of many curious histories, places, and persons.

With such prospects in view I ask you now, with book in hand, to lay aside for the brief time all ordinary cares and pleasures to dream with me, and withal to trust me as I lead you along from stage to stage. A novel, in order to

bear the truth of its name, must be novel, and
I promise that this shall open up a vision of
history new to a large majority and yet resting
on old realities, strangest of strange in the
past life of immortal races.   Yes, a history!
but differing from common history just as a
dream, founded on the reading of a real page
of modern matter of fact, might leave the in-
definite thought 'Did I dream it or hear it?'

FROM A BATTLEMENT.

A mighty encampment in Western Britain
stands near the spot where our vision is first
revealed.   It is the temporary home of armed
legions, who bend to the will of one man as
trees bend to the wind, gently, so gently they
are barely seen to move ; stately, so stately, as
if they were bowing their heads to a god of
war ; furiously, so furiously that lightning and
thunder, and hail and hurricane are combined
in a storm of destruction and death, clearing
all before them !

On the battlement of a tower built ages
after these legions were no more, we see, in
our vision, at the first glimpse, the lines of the

encampment of these men so well laid out and
so faithfully preserved, that all its parts are
easily filled up as the mind permits itself to
indulge in the effort.

The encampment is a square of eight
hundred yards on each side : a square with
earthworks for its ramparts, about fifteen feet
high on the inner side, and sloping so easily
that a man could run from the level to the
top at a breath. The ramparts are pierced
by four openings or portals, one commanding
each quarter of the heavens. The openings
are simply cut out of the earth ; there is neither
brick nor stone connected with them. Each
is closed, when required to be closed, by a
gate of massive wood, supported on huge
columns of wood or piles backed up by earth
and spanned over by a strong narrow bridge
also of wood, along which a solitary sentinel
silently paces, resting at intervals on his
spear, as if the spear with its shining point
aloft were a staff, held or fixed in its place
like a standard. As he rests he takes a
survey of the outer scene that lies beneath
him in tiers of external earthworks cut like
giant's steps one below another, and ending

at last in a deep incline which, in a descent
of five hundred feet, terminates gently in the
rugged plain from which the fortress takes its
rise.

Beneath the sentinels on the bridges span-
ning the gates we see other sentinels on the
terraces which surround the encampment.
These form a watchful circuit, every man true
to his beat as the path of a sun. As they
meet each other on relieving guard they
exchange a password which our ear, preter-
naturally acute, is permitted to catch. The
password is ' *Fidelis* ' of ' Cæsarea.'

At this moment, for some reason, the encampment is almost void of men. Men on
sentinel duty are there, but few other. Along
the main streets of the camp the sentinels, one
on each side, pass and repass in their measured
beats. Along the cross streets others do the
same, all of them on foot, but round the præ-
torium and chief officers' quarters, and, everywhere in the officers' part of the camp, the
sentries are mounted on horses noble as themselves. On the top of the ramparts, all round,
soldiers of a superior order hold the watch.
These are men of rather advanced years. They

have served their time, but have chosen to stay on, and they bear in their hands the javelin. They are the glory of the army ; they fill every post of solemn trust. They follow the commander of the camp whoever he may be, and on occasions of great ceremony surround him. They wear as their armour a headpiece of bright, almost white, metal, a shield of the same metal on their left arm, and a plate of it on their breast.

Intent as these various grades of guardians of the camp are on their duty, they are quick to listen, quick to hear ; and, as we detect, they often pause to catch any sound that may proceed from the south-western side of their encampment, beyond a little wood of pine-trees which skirts that spot and descends over the lower ramparts into the plain.

Our tower of observation, from which we get our look into the encampment, is itself built on a rising ground to the west of the camp. Once on its site stood a temple, dedicated to Apollo, traces of which yet remain beneath the present foundations, and even before then it had been a ruder temple of some previous

deity. Lost to both these, its first gods, it
was next transformed into a minster where
saintly devotees sang the early and the late
celebrations with the rising of the morn and
the closing of the night. And now for three
centuries it has been a simple parish church
standing alone in its glory, dear to its children
who worship in it the God of their fathers
and bury their dead under its shadows; dear,
very dear to the archæologist, as belonging to
four great epochs of human faith, worship,
architecture, and race.

From the eastern wall of the battlement
of this holy place we have looked, in our
vision, into the encampment lying so grandly
before us, and now we will move across to the
western wall to discover what is giving rise
below to the clamours to which the sentries
listen as they tread their rounds. But as we
pass from the eastern wall of the tower to the
western, we catch sight in the distance, on the
northern side, beyond a stretch of beautiful
country, of a steep white road dividing a long
and dense wood. This were a picture in itself
even if it were one of still life, still as death.
It is not still, for as we take the scene into

our mind we take also the fact that descending that hard white road there is a cavalcade in splendid marching order. As a bird would fly the cavalcade seems almost close upon us, although it is really some six or seven miles distant; for the road descends and afterwards winds amongst the trees of the valley below.

We discern that the members of the cavalcade are a mixture of horse and foot soldiers, the footmen in the centre marching nearly in a square, the horsemen before and behind in a longer and narrower line. The square of footmen appears to enclose some great treasure, as if it were moving with a citadel within it; but every part passes down the incline with an order and steadiness which is almost painful in its rigid regularity. The metal caps of the soldiers, their breastplates and the heads of their spears are dazzling from the brilliancy with which they reflect the rays of the sun; and so, like a train of silver, they descend into the depth that conceals them from our sight.

This diversion of our senses over, we turn now to take in the new view we were seeking, and nearly at our feet discover a gigantic amphitheatre crowded with spectators and marvellous to behold.

The amphitheatre is an enclosed space without ramparts, but laid out in some manner like the interior of the encampment. It is oblong in form, in which it differs from the camp, and on the low walls of it within are cut out tiers of seats raised one above another and grass-covered. In the centre, on the long side nearest to the camp, is a platform or daïs rounded in front so as to face the theatre and retreating backwards into a roadway which extends westward until it leads into the western gate of the encampment. The daïs is large enough to seat a hundred persons, and from the back of it rises the standard of the Roman eagle. Upon it are placed the seats of honour for the commander of the forces and his attendant officers. On the opposite side, and precisely facing the daïs, is another wide opening, a grand gateway through which, pro-bably, they who may be about to take part in the performances, contests, or speeches, may make their entrances and exits. Beyond that open gateway is the country, bounded in front by a low range of hills and farther back by mountains richly blue in colour and ending in one lofty peak which seems to crown the whole and shut off further view.

The place which lies immediately beneath us is the grand circus of the Roman Legions of Britain. A circus which every Roman soldier has heard of, and which many thousands have seen. A circus second only to that which Julius Cæsar built on Roman soil itself. It is half a mile in circumference, and will seat many thousand spectators.

In detail the circus of Britain resembles and yet differs from that of Rome. In it there is a path round which horses ridden by men as well as horses attached to chariots can race. In it the racers, combatants, or performers enter from the chief gateway opposite the daïs, and, marching across the arena by a path laid out for them, proceed to a smaller arena or ring immediately in front of the daïs, in which they carry out their minor combats or games under the immediate eye of the presiding genius of the fête ; or from which they file out into the large arena, when horsemen, swordsmen, runners or wrestlers are to

exhibit their mimic war or savage skill on a
grander scale.

The balconies of the circus are filled with
spectators, a mighty concourse of mixed
peoples wild with excitement if sounds may
be accepted as evidence of expectation.

Some great event is surely about to take
place, for observe the standards of the eagle
are being raised above the balconies at fixed
points; the centurions are placing their men
near each standard; and the trumpets are
giving forth a deafening voice.

Let us descend from our distant height
and find a place somewhere on the balconies.
Take care! that small ladder leading from the
door of the battlement to the beam below
which carries the bells is not too firm; the
beam is not too broad, and the next ladder
leading down to the belfry might be stronger
and steadier. It is well not to look down but
to keep the eyes turned towards the inside of
the tapering spire. All right, we are in the
belfry and the steps to the chancel are wind-
ing steps of stone, much worn but solid as
rocks. Never mind the darkness, it will last

but a moment ! We have reached the light,
and are through the low archway into the
open air !

IN THE CONCOURSE.

Come with me! Nothing save a field,
which we will quickly cross, lies between us
and the amphitheatre. Let us glide across,
skirting the path leading from the camp
to the daïs, but bearing a little to the right
that we may find a place in the balcony on
the left of the seats of honour. The magnates
from the camp have preceded us, and are
in their places by the time we have gained
our position, which fortunately commands a
splendid view of the whole scene and specially
of the General, who is seated like an Emperor
in the chair of state, and who is for the
moment the Emperor of western Roman
Britain.

We can now look round at leisure. We are
privileged ! To the whole assembly before us
we are unseen spirits, though they are not such
to us. We dream, and they are the world in
which, during the time of our vision, we are
cast.

CHAPTER II.

VIVAT FIDELIS!

By our side, as we survey the wonderful scene, are two men of quality whose conversation, as we are forced to hear it, tells us that they are newly arrived from Rome. Everything is as new to them as it is to us, if we may judge by their words. They are commenting on the differences of the Circus Britannicus and the Circus Maximus of Cæsar.

'Why is the spina,' meaning the low wall which ran nearly the whole length of the Roman circus, 'why, my Fabius, is the spina left out in this place?'

'Nay, I know not,' answers the companion of the questioner, 'nor why there is no meta,' referring to the raised pillar at each end of the spina which indicates the starting and finishing points of the Roman course.

They are interrupted at this moment by

a new arrival, who hastily climbs the balcony from the arena to greet them as strangers in Britain but as old comrades in Rome.

'By the gods it is Tinnius Rufus,' they both exclaim ere they proceed to salute their friend in the usual way with the kiss.

The person in question carries in his face the height of good humour. He is of ruddy complexion, and his beard and hair partake of the same bright glow. He is rather stout for his years, and his cheeks are roundly fat and full as well as ruddy. After the salutations they ask him the questions they have asked themselves.

'You wish to know, my Fabius, you wish to know, my Vibullius, why this circus, finished by the hands of these legions here is not in the Roman style. I will tell you. We found it, as we found the camp, ready for use. In ages to come the people will give us the credit of building hundreds of Roman camps and circuses in Britain, whereas we seized them all, planned and made by these island savages. This camp and amphitheatre we found in the best condition after we had wrested them from the people for whom, wishing to pacify them as much as possible, we have let the circus remain with the fewest possible changes. Here the natives still run their horses and chariots and men, in contests round the broad course. There, in the centre, where the earth rises they once filled wicker cages with their victims taken in war, and in honour of a sort of Apollo of their own burnt the wretches alive. In the fore, in front of our old schoolmate Julius Severus, who, as you see, has risen to the highest post here, is their lesser arena surrounded by a pit, in which they make their very cocks, armed on the claws with metal spurs, fight till, like other fools of heroes, they die immortal. Oh! by Mars, these ancient men of Britain knew how to play as well as fight. If in the days of Cæsar they had had Severus there to lead them, it is more likely they would have taken Rome than we their island.'

'Happy for us some good things have crept in,' responded Fabius. 'The calx (the chalk line) is there in order; the General sits in the tribune; the podium holds the officers; the noble horsemen have their proper places in the rear; the masters of the cere-monies are at their posts; and the Mappa (the

officer who throws down the white signal to
start each contest) is all alive. But where are
the judges?'

'Severus himself is sole judge in Britain.'

'It is just,' replied Fabius, with the slight
reverence which the cultured Roman offers
whenever the Emperor or his representative
is named. 'It is just, but I like not the
presence of those half-clad viragos in the
popularia' (the seats where the public find
places). 'In Rome the women of position alone
are permitted in the presence of the Emperor,
and they near to or around his person, or by
the side of the senate.'

'You do not understand these native
women, my Roman child,' responds the red
beard, 'or you would speak of them in different terms. They are not women, they are
demons. When Claudius made his way into
the east of the island, a woman who led the
people against him fought like a hundred
demons, and still her name is known and worshipped far and wide. Ten women out of
twenty are named after her. My own Boadicea
bears her name, and our daughter the same.'

'Eheu!' falters out Vibullius. 'Eheu! our

Tinnius has married a demon who heaps fire on his head. No wonder he should look so fierce.'

Here the conversation of the friends is stopped by the ring of the clarions, the rising of the vast multitude from their seats, and a general cry of the Roman people present:—

'The gods! the gods! the gods!'

At the cry Severus himself rises reverently from his throne, and now, for the first time, we distinctly perceive two separate and hostile races in occupation of the Circus Britannicus. It may be that the difference of dress and of costume distinguishes the races, for every Roman carries some sign of the conquering Roman soldier, while every native carries some sign of the subdued savage; it may be that the difference of build of body distinguishes them, for the Roman, close-built, sturdy-limbed, broad-faced, and round-headed, contrasts strongly with the tall, lithe, long-limbed body, and high, pointed, long head of the Briton. But the grand distinction is in the expression of the face of the two orders who make up the multitude, a distinction terribly declared when the clarions ring the order for the procession of the gods.

In one sense the procession is of living interest to both sets of spectators, for it heralds some great sights or contests which they are to behold, and which will stir their blood up to fever point. But to the Roman the procession is a solemn religious rite, whilst to the Briton it is a solemn mockery forced on him until it pierces him to the soul. The difference is as light to darkness.

The Briton has for ages worshipped the sun, the moon, and the stars ; his great god is one god who from earliest times has given himself to mankind as fire : who shows himself as the sun, and who is succeeded, when he withdraws his glorious face of gold, either by his child of silver the moon, or by night, the black demon of darkness and symbol of eternal death. To him, therefore, the worship of these sticks and stones, called gods, carried in their dumb and silly guises in chariots or on the shoulders of men, to which dumb things men bend their heads or prostrate their bodies, is idle show and play. The expression of the people tells their story of belief. The Roman reverently worships. The Briton, forced by the sword, performs the worship with an expression of hate, disgust, contempt, revenge, which no sword, however keen, can touch.

The faces of the subdued but not conquered people tell the everlasting story, that the mind of man is never, never vanquished. The faces declare as distinctly as the tongues could have told that the rulers of Britain with all their might have still a deadly enemy on their hands, an enemy they have for a moment coerced but have not finally suppressed : an enemy that will die but will never remain enslaved.

'The accursed gods,' murmurs a native chief to his wife, in their native tongue.

'Accursed!' hisses the woman between her teeth, like the sound of a serpent; 'I would we could burn them with their followers in the cages which once stood where the beasts now fight.'

'Silence!' calls out a Roman centurion, as with his vitis or rod of the vine, which a centurion always carries, he inflicts a deep mark first across the bare shoulders of the man and then of the woman; 'silence! and pay homage to the immortal gods!'

A groan, a curse, and a stiff-necked bend of the head as the images pass are the answers to this demonstrative command.

A suppressed cry from an almost adjoining seat calls attention to two figures so different to all the rest of the vast assembly and witnesses of the passing drama that they must surely belong to another and an unknown land.

A man and a child.

But for the intense anxiety to see what is to be exhibited in the arena, these two strangers would of themselves be centres of greatest attraction and wonder. They are neither Roman, British, Cymric, Gallic, nor Jewish; but wanderers who might have alighted from the skies.

The man is tall of stature, his countenance gentle as it is wise, his hair dark, his eyes blue. He is dressed in a garb itself sufficiently picturesque and novel to arrest the attention of the crowd near to him. Around his body is a closely fitting jacket or jerkin, with lappets artistically cut at the breast and throat so as to show a fold or roll which loosely encircles his neck. His lower limbs are enclosed in loose trousers which reach just below the knee and are gathered up with a silken girdle. The legs are clothed in long socks which extend to the knees, and are held in place beneath the trousers by the girdle of silk. The feet are hidden in shoes made of leather or hide, laced in front with golden cords and soled with some solid substance resembling the bark of a tree, the point of the shoe long and sharp. The jacket or body dress is supplemented by a mantle of emerald green, which, flowing over the under garments of almost yellow tint, gives a richness and chasteness of colour that is itself a picture. Finally, a head-dress consisting of a loose cap made of a substance like dark velvet, but of coarser texture, completes a costume as singular as it is convenient and graceful.

The companion of this strange being, obviously, both from look and from manner, his daughter, is, perhaps, more remarkable than himself. She may be sixteen years of age, but she retains all the innocence and beauty of the child. Her eyes, like those of her parent, are blue; her hair is a rich auburn, falling in precious curls which, wafted from

her brow over her shoulders, frame a face of
pale and saintly beauty. She is clothed in
one long dress of light yellow colour, gathered
in at the waist by a girdle of deeper colour,
and reaching to her feet which are clad in
sandals. Over her robe she, like her father,
wears a light mantle, also of emerald green.

As the sound of the first stripe of the
centurion catches her ear, she turns to learn
the cause, and seeing the cruel vitis descend
over the bare shoulders of one of her own
sex, her gentle heart gives way, and, with the
faint cry already noticed, she nestles closer
to the side of her protector, and in a tongue
peculiar to themselves implores, ' Father of
love, let us go hence ! let us go hence !'

' In good time, joy of my soul, but for the
moment we must keep still or they may strike
us also.'

The idea seems so awful to the angelic
child that she entwines her arm in his and
buries her head in the folds of his mantle.
But soon she summons up courage, and relying on that firm arm for support utters not
another word.

Whilst yet the red marks glow on the backs

of the offending natives, and whilst the stern
soldier looks on with contemptuous severity,
a new scene begins in which Briton and Roman
alike take eager part.

The trumpets ring out sharp and shrill,
the clarions bray, the cymbals clash from one
end to the other of the immense concourse.
In time the human voices take up the strain.
The voices shout in chorus to the trumpets,
in shrieks to the clarions, in laughter to the
cymbals.

An officer in authority by the side of Julius
Severus, the central figure of the scene, waves
aloft a white emblem, the starting-flag; the
musical instruments and voices cease their
clamour, and through the ranks, everywhere,
the lips of a hundred centurions ring out the
words :

'Sit down !   Sit down !'

Severus himself, who has been standing
and eagerly viewing the multitude before him,
is the first to obey.   He resumes with severe
dignity his vice-imperial throne.

And now all the throng is silent as the
grave.   So solid is every figure, every standard, every spear, it is as if the circus had

been stricken into a vast petrified sepulchre of men, women, and arms.

A moment of repose and the officer near to Severus, 'the Mappa,' lowers the white signal to indicate that something is about to be done.

Solemnly and with imposing ceremony there emerges from the gateway of the arena on the extreme right of the throne a chariot, hitherto concealed by a magnificent awning or tent, extending far along the road to the camp from the gateway. The chariot is of golden splendour, and soon to it fifty noble horses are attached in twenty-five pairs, while the same number, also in pairs, follow behind it. By each pair of horses stands a centurion. Across his breast, over his armour, a broad belt carries a long sword on his left side. From his girdle on his right side is suspended a short sword or dagger two spans long. His body armour reaches to his knees, leaving exposed below the powerful limbs and strongly sandalled feet. His left hand rests on the handle of the long sword ; his right grasps the vitis, or rod, which is peculiar to the rank of a centurion.

A soldier more thoroughly ready for victory or death it were indeed hard to find.

The rapidity with which these active men take their places on the left of the pairs of horses they have to govern is in itself a marvel of mechanical life. The horses and men are ready to move at a word.

Men and horses form three long lines, each straight as an arrow.

Severus nods approval, and ' when Severus approves all men may be satisfied.' So runs the saying from lip to lip, respecting the man who takes his name from his nature, Julius the Severe.

Not a bridle, not a halter, is fitted to the finely trained horses which draw or follow the chariot; a light leathern collar chastened with silver encircles their stately necks, and on each side from it a silver cord acting as a trace connects one horse to the other and the leaders to the chariot; the vitis and the voice of each master are alone sufficient to lead these brave and intelligent animals anywhere, to sport, to fight, to triumph, to death.

The eyes of the horses follow those of their masters, who, bare-headed, move on in one living and unbroken form, one mechanism, one movement, one mind.

The savage Briton, still writhing under his punishment, cannot withhold his admiration.

'Oh Throth the everlasting,' he mutters to himself, 'why lettest thou these brazen heads learn to control, by magic, the noblest servant thou hast created for those who serve thee?'

The chariot so magnificently horsed and tended is strangely occupied.

It is a chariot of the true Roman style, but somewhat larger than those in common use. It is borne on two low wheels, is entered from behind, and is rounded in front in order to afford convenient space for the driver.

But this time no driver is needed, and none is there.

In the centre of the floor of the chariot, upright as a dart, immovable, his left hand resting on his sword-handle, his right hand holding the vitis, stands another centurion, in each and every respect like one of the leaders of the horses, except that he is more majestic than any of them, that his head is bare, and that from his left shoulder a sagum, or military cloak, falls gracefully on his left side.

To him this day is the event of his life; for to his especial honour this festival of gods and men is devoted.

And, posed like a pillar of the State, he claims the honour naturally, as an honour rightfully and worthily won.

He is not, however, alone in his splendour. At his feet, her back resting against the fore part of the chariot, in the graceful curve of it, there sits a female figure. Is she a child, a girl, a woman?

Let it be assumed that she is a woman, but very young.

Her rich black hair is trimmed into the shape of a helmet. It is a crest overhanging a brow beneath which the eyes of an eastern face, eyes of darkened fire, sparkle like gems in a cave. She is clothed in the stola or woman's toga, differing from the Roman male toga in that its edges are fringed. The stola is of the purest white, the stola of the festival, like the surplice of a priest, except that a light but flowing girdle somewhat tightens it to her body. Her feet are clad in white slippers, which complete her attire.

In her right hand this companion of the mighty centurion bears a mystical emblem dedicated to Apollo. This banner she holds aloft by a white wand. It is round like the sun, and on its face, on each side, bears the radiant image of that luminary in rays of gold on a surface of red. In its centre are three letters, in the Greek character, the sacred symbol, meaning that the god has an existence or being, and that all the children of men, and all created beings, are animated by his light and his life.

As the last pair of horses are attached to the chariot, and as the cortège begins to move in procession round the course, the deeply suppressed silence bursts forth into tumult. Three times round the course the cortège slowly passes, and each time with increasing excitement. In the stir it is hard to view calmly the hero of the hour or his companion, but by patient waiting they are revealed.

He is a soldier of soldiers. He stands like a rock in a raging sea of life, unmoved and unmoveable, and his manner is followed by his companion with equal serenity. The cold piercing glance of Severus touches neither of them, nor the scream of the virago, nor the gestures of the three Roman friends who discuss the sight.

'He bears himself,' observes Vibullius, 'as if he were going into battle.'

'Nay,' suggests the classical Fabius, 'he goes as if he were about to meet the Council of Minds in the Heavens of the illustrious dead.'

'Or,' put in the much married Tinnius, 'as if he were about to face his wife.'

If these were tests of merit, and if he concerning whom they were spoken were bent on proving them as such, he did indeed win all the praise he earned.

'A fig for the Council of Minds and the native Tinua of Tinnius; a fig for the man in the chariot and all his fame; the woman, the woman for me!' ejaculated Vibullius. 'She is worth twenty of the man, she is a centurion of a woman and one in a thousand. But who, my hen-pecked, rubicund Tinnius, who, by Venus and the mother of the gods, is she?'

The excited Tinnius is too intent at the

moment to answer this eager and natural question, and before it can be repeated a new event has occurred which seizes the attention of all who are near at hand and, in some degree, of the spectators generally, including the keen-eyed Severus.

As the chariot passes for the third time the place where the stranger man and his child are seated the bearer of the sacred emblem in the chariot turns, by accident, her face towards them.

It is the merest accident, the merest glance, a glance on strangers of strangers to her!

What is there in a glance? We bring a loadstone near to a particle of steel, a suspended needle: the point of the needle may fly to the magnet; ah no! it flies from it. Why?

The puzzle is but partially solved, so is the puzzle of a glance. The glance may be love; ah, no! it may be hate. It may be trust, or courage; ah no! it may be distrust or awe; it may be surprise or wonder.

In this case, as the dark eyes of the woman in the chariot receive, through the distance, the glances from the blue eyes of those strangers they excite in her a double impression.

The eyes of the angelic child excite wonder, intense and startling ! While the eyes of the protector of the child excite awe ; for the first time in all her life, awe ; awe, sudden and incomprehensible.

The emblem of Apollo falls on the knees of its bearer.

' Apollo goes down in the noontide of his glory,' observes Fabius, ' 'tis a bad omen.'

And, such is the influence of the omen on the minds of the Roman people, that there is not a Roman there, from the camp servant to the vice-imperial Severus, who does not feel the vibration, with one exception.

The exception is the centurion of the chariot. He, with his eyes fixed in space, heeds not, and, gathering resolution from his iron will, the bearer of the emblem, raising her hand to put back a wandering lock of hair which has fallen over her brow, lifts up the banner again, in graceful movement, as if the whole had been a mere natural act on her part, an act intended and harmonious with her duty.

The skilful diversion is rewarded with a

new burst of applause, which, coming after a pause of silence, is a proof of success. Rome is itself again ! And now once more the inquisitive Vibullius returns to his speculation. Who is this woman of women, and who is this man of men ? Who are they both that they should excite so much admiration ? They are not patricians he knows, why then are they so honoured ?

There is vanity, as usual, in the thought which fills Vibullius. 'Here am I,' it says silently, ' I Vibullius, one of the most ancient of the great families of Rome, before whom that Julius Severus is a mere mushroom, and the Emperor himself but a plant of a single season at the best. Here am I, unknown and unhonoured, while these two plebs of plebs, and one of them an eastern mockery, a slave it may be, or a creature of Severus, are treated like gods ! I must know who and what they are.'

His curiosity has not long to wait, for ere he can return to the task of questioning the Red-beard, the chariot stops before the seat of Severus ; the twenty-five pairs of the foremost horses are detached from it and are moved forward on the course, to stand at some little distance from the chariot; and, the shrill blast of the trumpet from the back of the daïs is calling the lookers-on once more to silence.

Complete order restored, Severus descends from his throne, and stepping forward to the edge of the daïs close to which the chariot is drawn, rests his right foot on the edge of the chariot and places, amidst a storm of trumpets, clarions, cymbals, and voices, a chaplet of laurel on the head of the centurion.

In a moment all is still, as Severus returns to his seat.

At the sign of the commander, the Public Orator, the renowned Saserna, whose voice could shake the camp, stands forth. In his left hand he bears a scroll, in his right hand a spear held firmly like a staff.

What he has to declare is again heralded by the voice of the trumpet, from which he seems, by some clever art, to attune his own voice as musicians set their lutes to a tuning-fork, so that the note of the trumpet and the voice of Saserna hold on the sound into articulate words which all can hear. And so,

in the language first of Rome and then of
Britain, he delivers his message :—

'The army, Rome, and the Emperor,
through Julius Severus, Governor of Siluria
in Britain, confer a crown of honour on
Fidelis of Cæsarea, a centurion, who after
eight decades of noble service, devoted to
the Gods, to Rome, to Cæsar, and to Glory,
reaches his hundredth year of Life.'

'*Vivat Fidelis!*'

CHAPTER III.

MAN AND BEAST.

'VIVAT FIDELIS! Vivat Fidelis!' rings again and again, and still the centurion of a hundred years is unmoved in his place. But enthusiasm, like all else that is human, must die, and in time this great demonstration passes into silence. The horses before and behind the triumphal chariot are separated in pairs and led away, until one pair alone remains to draw the chariot and those that are in it towards the vestibule from which it first emerged into the public view.

As the last sign of the centurion disappears Severus and those around him retire for an interval into a tent at the back of the daïs over which the Roman standard proudly floats.

And now, waiting for the next event, the great assembly reposes.

Meantime the armed attendants clear the arena, and prepare for some momentous and thrilling spectacle.

The faces of the masses begin to resume their respective characteristics : the Roman faces are eager ; the Britannic are savage; the Jewish—for there is a fair sprinkling of Jewish blood in the audience—solemn and sad.

Severus is again in his place, the signal is given and the procession of the gods once more makes its round.

' What next have they in store for us ? ' the comrades of Tinnius Rufus ask eagerly and with one voice.

' A battle, a battle ! A battle between wolves, a bear and a boy !'

' Say rather between wolves, a fiend of darkness, and an angel of light,' sighs one who sits near, and hears the question and answer it has evoked.

The speaker speaks in the Roman tongue but with a foreign accent ; and, though his words are clearly understood, they come forth with so much emotion they almost choke him on their way.

' Judaicus, a Jew,' whispers Tinnius. ' It

is one of his tribe that is about to compete in the arena.'

' A Jew in Britain!' ejaculates Vibullius in an undertone. ' Turn wherever we may and these dogs are to be found. Jews in Britain, indeed!'

' I tell you,' continues Tinnius, leading his friends a little higher up the balconies, ' there are thousands of them, and here they flock most; for, after the taking of their holy city, during the reign of Vespasian, they wandered everywhere, and in these Silurian mountains and caves met with a native race which took to them so kindly that they have become quite numerous here, and, from the coasts about, have opened trade with the Phœnicians of Tyre and Sidon. It is the policy of Severus, generally, to be at peace with the creatures, for they roll in money, and, too obstinate for deep friendship, are hard to please.'

' And who is this one of their race who is going to give us a treat of his metal?' asks Fabius. ' Can they fight as well as they can barter?'

' You shall see. This is one of them: a youth whom Fidelis the centurion brought with him from Cæsarea, a slave whom he had freed some think, but not all !'

'I dare say not, thou winking ferret,' breaks in Vibullius; 'but why should he be called into the arena if he be, as thou suggestest, the centurion's flesh and blood? What hath he done that he should make sport for wolves and savages?'

'He hath passions during which his tongue hath declared his hatred of Rome. He hath refused to offer incense to Cæsar, or even to lay incense on the altar of Ceres when her richest harvest in Britain, in the memory of man, called for her festival.'

'But there he comes. Judge for yourselves!'

'He comes as anything but a slave. By Apollo, he comes like a rising sun!' exclaims Fabius, as the youth of whom they speak is led before the august presence of the vice-Emperor.

'A rebellious Syrian,' murmurs the Red Beard.' I would I could wring his stiff neck as I liked!'

'A noble child, who fears no hand of man and obeys none but the Holy One of Israel,'

communes the Jewish sympathiser who spoke
a short time before. 'May the God of
Abraham, Isaac, and Jacob be with him, as
he promised to our forefathers Abraham and
his seed for ever. Amen.'

The prayer of this Israelite—'Aaron of the
Altar' by name amongst his own, 'Porcus'
a pig, amongst the Roman people—is echoed
silently by many of his race who in various
disguises are present.

He, Aaron, being a freedman, has no occasion for disguise; he is reputed to be so rich
that Severus himself is oftentimes his debtor.
But even he has to be careful of his words
and acts for the sake of his people, whom it is
his destiny to govern in silent government. He
is their father; he reads to them in secret
the sacred law; he proves and confirms them
in their faith ; he settles their differences; he
marries their young people according to ancient rite ; he keeps before them the name
and word and promise of the Mighty One of
Israel, and teaches them, in that holy name,
to believe that though they walk through the
valley of the shadow of death, he, the Mighty
One, is with them ; that his rod and staff shall

guide them ; that his kingdom is at hand; and that the Roman power shall have no permanent hold on the children of Zion.

And still, wise as the serpent, gentle as the dove, he advises them to pay homage unto Cæsar, and even lay incense on the pagan altars, lest for their unnecessary obstinacy, they perish by fire, cross, or sword.

He is indeed wise, and his people know him as if he were the chief of chief Rabbis in this foreign, distant, isolated land.

He pronounces his prayer, for the youth before the daïs, with his eyes bent to the earth ; but the sound of the first clarion makes him raise them and cast them on the type of his race, who so proudly and defiantly stands forth for fate.

'Oh, brave but foolish child !' he mentally laments, 'oh, bold but reckless Simeon of my people ! Why didst thou not bend in body to these tyrants ? Why didst thou not take heed to thy ways, and offend not with thy tongue ? Why didst thou refuse counsel of him whose royal blood is in thy veins ? "Be not righteous overmuch, neither make thyself overwise !" Why shouldest thou destroy thyself? Why shouldest thou die before thy time?'

Meanwhile, he who is thus commented on by Aaron of the Altar and a hundred men of his race, remains standing in simple majesty. Brought out for the sport of a savage multitude, his young life at stake, he of all seems most exalted and commanding. Severus on high, in his viceregal seat, clad in imperial robe, the white toga with purple border, surrounded by his six lictors bearing their fasces or rods, the standard of the Roman empire overshadowing him, and the sword, the spear, and saddle of Roman knighthood at his feet, even he seems to feel the common spell of admiration, as bending down to his nearest attendant he enquires :

'Of what doth this contest consist?'

'The youth, a Jew, most noble Severus, who stands before you armed with the short sword which he holds in his left hand, but which he uses with either hand with equal dexterity, is to be turned into the small arena, surrounded by the deep pit, in company with the Numidian bear belonging to the centurion Milo and six famishing wolves. The bear, armed with a huge club for a weapon, is to engage the wolves with the Jew, and, if they two despatch the wolves, they are themselves to fight with club and sword till one is killed. The victor is then to be at the disposal of the people.'

'It is a new sport,' observed Severus in a tone and manner implying that this is the first he has heard respecting the combat or the combatants.

And still Simeon the Jew stands as a model of masculine beauty and godlike life.

He is five feet nine inches in height, and in body and limb of fine proportion. He wears on his body a closely fitting leathern jerkin, with a light tunic suspended from it and reaching to the knees. The tunic is held up by a red sash, which fits like a belt and falls negligently in two loose ends or tassels on his left side. His arms, excessively powerful, but almost white in colour and shaped like those of a woman in respect to symmetry and outline, are entirely free; his lower limbs, equally well formed and strong, are girt only in a light sandal, the thong of which is fancifully twisted around the ankle and a short distance up the leg.

His head is uncovered, except for its rich raven hair which hangs in clusters at his back down to his shoulder-blades, and is parted from his forehead over the exact centre of the crown of the head. His face, of striking cast, with pointed chin, aquiline nose, piercing dark eyes, long arched dark eyebrows meeting at the centre, and a broad though retreating forehead, is the perfected image of the perceptive, ready, fearless, resolute, reckless spirit that animates the whole frame of the man with living fire. On him, thus standing before the Roman chief, undaunted and bright of countenance, the British woman, still smarting from the vitis, looks with more of admiration than prudence, a state suddenly checked by the aspect and growl of her jealous lord, who, tolerating from her no admiration that is not expended on his own uncouth self, shows his teeth dangerously.

The trumpet proclaims a new arrival and a new step in the coming drama.

Along the grand path of the circus, towards the ring facing the daïs, Milo the centurion leads, by a light chain, the second combatant, the Numidian bear.

The audience, from Severus to the lowest slave, is startled with delight or with wonder. Whether it be really a bear or a man disguised as a bear is the puzzle.

The excitement is such that wagers begin to be laid on the point.

'I wager a flagon of red wine it is a bear,' exclaims the excited Vibullius. 'See thou its head, its ears, its big eyes, its huge frame?'

'I take the wager willingly,' returns the calmer Fabius, ' and to-night we will drink it with song and story. I stand by the feet, the hands, the limbs, which, covered with bear hide though they be, are human. Besides, seest thou not the height of the beast? No bear standeth that height, a head or more above the handsome Jew, who is of good pro-portion; his walk also is that of a man, and mark how he holds that fearful club as if it were a javelin or a spear. A bear would hug the thing close to its body, not push it forth at arms' length like that.'

At this moment all the mystery vanishes. By a jerk of his body the Numidian bear throws back the head-piece of the animal as if it were a hood, and stands declared a man, with a human head and face stained dark as the hairy skin which clothes his body.

He is indeed a sight of terror. His own hair stands erect; his large fierce eyes roll in fury from side to side; his nostrils dilate; his red lips are curled apart, showing rows of large teeth white as snow and round and regular as those of any beast of the field; his ears, naturally large, he moves at will; while by an action of the muscle of the head and forehead he possesses the power of drawing down his hair until it seems to touch his eyebrows and then of lifting it back until all the fore part of his head looks actually bald.

To the infinite delight of the spectators before whom he stands, he goes through these gestures at the command of his master, until weary of the sight they crave for some new pastime.

In form the creature is massive, yet well shapen; his body is finely proportioned, his limbs, as far as can be judged of them covered as they are with bear-skin, are large, strong, and lissom; the nails of his fingers and toes are long and claw-like.

As to costume he wears but the one garment, the veritable skin of a huge black bear. His arms are thrust through the skin in which the upper limbs of the original animal played : his legs are thrust through the similar parts of the hinder limbs. Over the fore part of the body the skin is lashed with leathern thongs. As already seen, the bear's head is now thrown back like a hood, while a small bushy tail at the nether extremity forms a ludicrous protuberance, which wags with every movement, and excites the wildest laughter when nothing serious intervenes to change the general humour.

At another order from his master the human monster exhibits his prowess with his club, a weapon which reaches to the height of his chin, and which, thick as his own thick arm at its further end, tapers down towards its handle in even and regular form. Made of a hard dark wood, like solid oak, the weight of this weapon is amazing, yet the creature wields it as if it were a reed. Loosened, by Milo, from his chain, he steps backward a few paces further from Severus, and, after kneeling on one knee in reverence, rises, and by an upward jerk casts the club straight into the air many feet,

like a dart, and waiting for its fall, which
seems to be directed, inevitably, towards the
top of his own head, catches it by its handle
as it falls before him, ere it touches the
ground ; then, whirling it fiercely above his
head, he flings it from him in a long curve,
full twenty yards, and rushing after it catches
it again before it falls.

The multitude howl with delight, and
when, in another new feat, the monster seizes
the handle of the club with both hands, spins
it round and round, until by the momentum
it carries his body with it with such rapidity
that he and it resemble a wheel—himself the
centre and the thick end of the club the
circumference—the fury mounts to delirium ;
the cymbals strike in, the clarions bray, and
the trumpets ring in wild and indescribable
confusion.

With perfect ease and with marked grace
he makes the revolving wheel stop, and order
is restored.

And now the combatants are placed face
to face before Severus, ten paces apart, ready
at a sign from the Mappa to begin the combat which they have to face.

At the sign from the Mappa, a cage of a curious construction winds along the grand path. It is an iron cage in which six famishing wolves are confined. The noise from them alone is sickening, and the expression of their fierce despair, as they thrust their muzzles and their paws through the bars of the cage, is appalling to witness.

Severus himself affects not to see them ; the Mappa turns away as if about to give a direction to some one in the rear of him ; Tinnius and his friends stop their ears, and the Romans generally are not particularly pleased. But the native Britons rejoice. The wolf is their native natural enemy. To hunt the beast, to kill him, to carry his head to the chief, and to receive the reward for the same is the perfection of sport.

No better game could the Roman tyrants have selected for the children of Britain than the killing of wolves by man. Two men to six wolves ! It is beyond admiration.

The small arena or ring is two hundred yards in circumference. It is surrounded by a deep pit fifteen feet wide, from the edge of which, and pointing to the centre, a few inches

apart, stand out a double row of pikes, forming
a fence of iron palisade and rendering escape
from the arena impossible, or as it would seem
impossible. And yet every one can see any
sport going on within the circle.

A narrow bridge of earth, just wide enough
to allow for the passage of the cage, separates
the small arena from the daïs. The two human
victims are to be led into the centre of this ring.
They are to be followed by the cage of wolves.
The cage is to make, slowly, the complete
circuit within the circle, and brought partly
out of the narrow gateway of the bridge is
to fill up the passage. Then the back of the
cage is to be let down, and remaining as a
fence to the bridge, the furious brutes are to
be allowed to leap into the arena and kill, or
be killed by, their human assailants.

'Another wager, another flask of rich red
wine, if on this savage island it can be obtained,'
cries Vibullius; 'another wager, this time on
the wolves and the bear; an amphora, if you
like, an amphora!'

'I back willingly the young Jew against
all the beasts,' responds Fabius gravely. 'The
gods favour beauty.'

'But not his gods; they, 'tis said, delight in no man's beauty. I back the wolves and the glorious bear.'

'So let it be and let Tinnius hold the stakes, if he is sure his wife will not steal them ere he joins us at the settlement.'

'No fear, no fear, my comrades,' exclaims the delighted Red Beard. 'I'll bury them until nightfall, when we will reclaim them and bury them again in our own skins. Moreover, we shall have something to talk about, for this will be a combat of combats, one, if I mistake not, to be remembered for ages in Britain and related even in Rome. If the men beat the wolves, they are to fight until one of them falls, and after that the conqueror is still to be at the will of the people.'

And, such is the barbarous soul of all-conquering Rome, that they to whom this news is conveyed, they, sons of the highest and most accomplished families of the empire, they, men of refinement and culture, as they rank amongst their peers, receive the information with the simple, cruel, gratified observation:

'It is good!'

CHAPTER IV.

AVE CÆSAR!

ONCE more the trumpets ring out. The two human victims, for such they are, are being led forth, the cage of wolves is following, and the multitude is raised to such excitement that the minutes seem hours.

The Mappa is preparing to raise the signal. He has attached it to a cord, in order that he may draw it up to the top of a staff, that all may see it and observe the moment when it shall fall and the wild beasts be set free into the ring.

The silence that precedes this final act seems to be felt by the wild beasts themselves, as if they knew their prey was at hand, and their cravings were about to be satisfied.

The silence is more distressing than the clamour! But the signal is rising and suspense will soon cease!

The spell is broken, not by the fall of the

expected signal, towards which so many eyes
are turned, but by a loud clang and noise in
the rear of the daïs. Severus, who is leaning
forward eagerly intent as the rest, starts as
though he had been struck in the back.

He has not recovered his surprise when a
messenger approaches him, and, with knee
bent to the floor, presents to him a missive or
despatch. Severus breaks the seal, reads with
wild wonder; then speaks to the Mappa, and
evidently issues some new command, for that
important officer straightway raises his wand
as an intimation that hostilities must wait.

A moment more and Saserna, the Orator,
after conference also with Severus, stands
before the people, and with his trumpet-
voice proclaims :—

'Let the combats be suspended, and the
sport remain as it is until the signal for it be
again given. And, let no one move from the
place he occupies on penalty of death.'

The voice ceases, the multitude composes
itself to a fearful suspense, not one daring even
to move until Severus, who, with a sad and

humiliated expression on his kingly face, rises, and, followed by his lictors, officers and standard-bearer, retires from the scene into the pavilion leading from the daïs.

'Silence! silence! silence! silence! in the four quarters of the amphitheatre. Silence!'

By an order to the men in charge of the cage of wolves, the cage is drawn back along the path whence it came, and out of sight and hearing. But the human victims are left near the gate of the enclosure, face to face. In time the tone and temper of the great audience affects them, and they also turn their eyes to the daïs, and join in the common wonder.

At last expectation is rewarded. A band of centurions, Fidelis of a hundred years at their head, make their appearance on the daïs, and under his direction form into two lines with a wide path between their ranks.

And now through the open space, on the way to the seat of state, there comes a new procession.

The maiden of the chariot and companion of Fidelis leads the way, dancing the most exquisite of dances to the clashing of cymbals which she holds above her head, until she reaches the front of the throne, before which she gracefully casts herself almost at full length upon the ground.

She is followed by a soldier, bare-headed, in marching order, carrying his sword: a man of scarcely middle age, fresh, evidently, from a long march, and distinguishable only from the ordinary Roman soldier by one and singular mark of distinction.

At his back a tall slave bears on the staff of a spear, over his head, a diadem of gold, and from time to time whispers in his ear some solemn injunction.

They who are near can catch the words :—

'Remember that thou art but a man.'

'By all the gods!' exclaims the astonished Fabius to his friends, 'it is——'

His sentence is cut short by the trumpet blast and voice of Saserna from the left of the throne :—

'To your knees all men, women, and children! Let every knee bend to the earth to Cæsar.'

In an instant the multitude obeys, all but the two combatants and he to whom the homage is paid; from Severus on his right hand to the meanest slave; each and all bend to the earth before this human deity.

The Emperor Hadrian!

At this solemn moment the three men remaining erect form a triangle; a Jew, of noble bearing and beauty, and a disfigured Slave of gigantic build form the angles of its base; while the Prince of all the civilised world forms its apex.

There is something fearfully strange in the sight of a mighty mass of human beings in one fixed attitude, and to Hadrian, impressionable almost to madness, this vast crowd prostrate at his feet is the strangest event of his romantic life. He is moved even to tears, and clutches his sword as if to find support.

His eyes fall on the two extraordinary beings who, like himself, stand erect above the prostrate humanity, and his soul is disquieted in a way akin to fear. A strange thought crosses his mind: 'To whom do all these creatures bend, to me, or to one of these make-sports; to me, or to that youth who stands like Apollo ; or to that giant who stands like Hercules ? ' Then, as he scans the face and figure of the youth, he trembles. It is a face he has never seen before, yet he knows it : the face turns as if to give him another view of it. He knows it better, and is perturbed the more. The face strikes him both with admiration and affection. It cannot be, but it is :—

'Would that he were my son,' is the sentiment which, unbidden, rises in his breast.

It may be merely the sigh of a childless man. There are such sighs, and this is from the heart, as they ever are.

He must not wait now either to philosophise or to lament; those bending forms must be set free. Already they have been constrained too long.

The Emperor takes his seat, and at a breath from his lips the word of command follows :—

'It is the will of Cæsar that the people rise, and that the combat commence at the proper signal.'

The order also goes forth by signs that the cage of wolves be recalled.

Meanwhile, to fill up the interval, the Numidian bear is brought before the Emperor, and, at command from Milo, once more goes through his wondrous feats of skill.

To Hadrian the whole scene is novel of novel. Arrived but lately in Britain, and travelling by rapid marches since the day of his disembarkation at Dola on the eastern side of the Island, he has seen no signs of sports, nor, indeed, any evidences of a civilised community. A Circus Maximus such as this is therefore to him a surprise. The modifications of the plans of the circus, the faces of the people, the customs, are all further novelties on which for a passing moment he is inclined to dwell.

'What,' asks he of Severus, who is now seated on his right hand, 'what is the nature of the coming combat?'

In briefest terms the Vice-Ruler tells him the nature of it, and of the two men who are to share in it.

'And which,' he asks, 'is the most skilful?'

'They are of such different bloods, great Prince,' returns Severus, 'I dare not wage.

The youth, a Jew called Simeon, exalted by a
visionary enthusiasm, is filled with the idea
that, pre-ordained by the gods, or rather his
God, for great glory, he cannot be killed or
die, but, like one of his ancestors, will be
received into heaven in a chariot of fire.
To this he adds skill and agility with the
short sword. The Numidian, on the other
hand, relies on his strength, the strength of
Hercules himself. He has never yet failed
to break with that ponderous club every bone
in the body of his enemy.'

'Is he without fault?' asks Hadrian, who
is quick to feel general impressions of faults
which others do not perceive, a faculty on
which he greatly prides himself.

'He is said to have one fault, for which
his late master sold him cheaply to Milo, the
centurion there, whose property he now is.'

'Some failure of sight or of limb?'

'No, Prince, he hath no fault of that
nature, as you may deduce from what you have
witnessed. He handles his club as if it were
a javelin; but he is said to be possessed of a
demon who at times throws him to the earth,
tears him so that he raves, becomes hideous

of expression, gasps for life, foams at mouth, pierces his flesh with his talons, and bites his tongue almost at wain.'

' Enough! enough!' ejaculates the Emperor, ' such an one were best dead. Were it the will of Jove that the damned spirit which inhabits these creatures could die with them, I would that youth's sword were deep in the monster's heart. Unhappily, the accursed thing leaves one body only to enter another. But who is this maiden at my feet?'

' Her Jewish and real name as I have heard is Huldah, after a prophetess of her people. But in the camp she passes as Fidelia, because Fidelis, a centurion, who is a hundred years old to-day, and in whose honour this festival is held, bought or found her, as well as the youth Simeon, during the reign of Trajan.'

' Is she also inspired?' asks the still more startled Emperor.

' In a different way ; she forecasts events ; breaks forth suddenly into music and song, as you, Prince, have witnessed ; heals wounds, cures the sick, and withal wields the sword and casts the javelin like a trained soldier.'

' By Bacchus ! noble Prætor, methinks thou

art in love with the maiden, for which I blame
neither thy taste nor thy judgment; yet tell
me one thing more : mine eyes seize in the
distance the figures of a noble man and a child
of immortal beauty. Are they from the skies?'

'They are strangers, Prince. A chief and
a child, as I have but just learned, of the
western island of Juverna, on which Roman
foot never stood; the Island, so-called, of
Peace and Beauty.'

'I knew not that the whole world possessed
such a spot,' sighs the ruler of the world. 'I
would I were there! Meantime let the combat open, and see to it that in the evening I
hold converse with this wondrous chieftain.'

CHAPTER V.

A MIRACLE.

To show the due reverence to the powers of heaven by the powers of earth, the procession of the gods once more advances as preliminary to the contest of men with beasts.

The ceremony duly celebrated, the human victims are led into the ring. The cage of wolves follows; it makes its way slowly round and comes back to the entrance. It is drawn by eight men, two abreast; a single pole, a shaft with four crossbars attached to it breast-high, forms the means by which the men, who are professed wolf-trainers, propel the machine along.

As they reach the narrow portal of the ring they leave the cage or wolf-chariot in the gap; then their leader, by means of an iron rod, lets down the back of the cage, his men lift up the pole, and the wolves are tilted out

on to the green sward of the ring. The brutes
roll over each other, and for a moment fight
with each other: they recover themselves, re-
gain their feet, and form a circle, their noses
almost touching.

'They are holding a council of war, the
brutish beasts,' observes Vabullius.

'Not worse than a human council,' is the
reply of Fabius.

'Hark! the council is over; they have
determined on attack.'

A perfectly fiendish howl of the beasts,
with their heads in the air, declares this fact.

'They are invoking their gods,' continues
the rude Vibullius. 'Oh, gods of wolves! hear
their prayer, for I have backed them to my
last coin.'

The two men in the ring are as different
in their proceedings as if they were from a different sphere. The attitude of the Numidian
is one of watchful zeal to protect, apparently,
not himself so much as his comrade.

'He is not going to let the wolves kill
Simeon, if they dared,' muses Aaron of the
Altar.

'He is reserving the honour of that

achievement to himself,' thinks Severus; and so think many more.

As to Simeon, he seems to care no more than if he were strolling in a garden.

In time the wolves form a semicircle towards the men, who stand back at the far edge of the ring near to the pit, but facing the daïs.

Gradually and stealthily they close in on the men, who can retreat no further, as if at one spring they will seize their limbs and throats and finish them straightway.

They are interrupted in their scheme by the Numidian, who, with club raised, rushes towards the centre of the foe, and, leaping clean over the two brutes in the centre, turns back, and, with deadly blows dealt right and left, lays two of his fiercest enemies helpless at his feet.

They two are now easy prey: the mighty club puts them quickly out of all their misery.

The native Briton rubs his hands with glee. 'There is not a bone in the body of the beasts that is not smashed. This is sport, indeed!'

'Two of the wild beasts gone,' reckons the silent but less pleased Severus.

'By what spell is that Jew protected?' wonders Hadrian; for the four remaining wolves, all but surrounding Simeon, seem to lie down at his bidding.

He makes no defence, except that with arms folded he looks at them with a serene pity as unworthy of his regard.

'Why, maiden, do they not tear him limb from limb?'

'Because he is beloved of his God.'

Another question, about to follow, is stopped by a new turn of affairs in the ring. The beasts, diverting their gaze from Simeon, wheel round on the Numidian, and, making a desperate spring at him, give him bare time to escape. One of them is indeed successful in gripping and tearing off the head of the bear and a piece of the skin which covers his body, and finding it eatable, commences to devour it. The three others follow him in quick pursuit, but, entirely master of the situation, the Numidian, anxious to be the sole victor, outruns them, literally plays with them, leaps over them, and, finally, in turn chases them. By a dexterous hurl of his club he levels one to the ground as they are flying before him ; he picks up his weapon, and, dismissing this enemy, takes the other two at leisure. They are the weakest of the group, and have been famished too long to hold their strength ; they crawl in fear, and in tender mercy are destroyed with a single blow.

'Five out of six gone,' reckons Severus and the rest, who believe that Simeon will be the last victim.

It promises so. Before the Numidian and his club there remain but two foes : the wolf still engaged on the head of the bear, which furnishes a wonderful meal, and the beautiful youth, armed, ready, and matchless in skill, courage, and endurance.

There is now a general cry : 'The beasts no more. The men ! the men ! the men !'

The Numidian heated with his exertions, and wilder than ever in his appearance, is ready for the work ; he will clear the way for his final contest by killing that last and feasting wolf, feasting under the very eyes of Hadrian.

Stealthily and rapidly he advances to the

greedy brute, too intent on its meal to heed its danger. The club swings nearly to the ground over the back of its master, in order that he may give with more effect the full and shivering blow; when, as if overbalanced by the weight of his weapon, with a wild and unearthly shriek he falls back upon it, and from head to foot writhes in convulsive struggles. The veins of his neck grow turgid; his face grows dark; he gasps for air; he foams at his mouth; his eyeballs roll wildly until the white part is alone visible; and he utters sounds and gurgles which no one understands.

With a swift movement the Emperor and the vast multitude rise to their feet, more terror-stricken by this sight than by all they have seen before, though it had been twenty times intensified.

Terror of the supernatural takes the place of the excitement of a natural scene to them far more fearful.

The Emperor's prejudgment is correct.

The monster man is faulty; he is possessed of a demon.

The wolf that has devoured the half meal it so fortunately won is quick to perceive another meal at hand. In an instant it had torn open the breast of the Numidian but for an interposition.

The hand of Simeon grasps the creature by the neck, and holds it like a tamed or cowed dog trying to escape and fly whither it may.

And now a new wonder!

Huldah, from resting on her knees survey-ing the scene at the feet of Hadrian, rises majestically and proceeds to the help of the possessed man.

The wolf-trainers at a sign from her remove the cage which forms the barrier, that she may enter the arena.

To the side of the possessed man she glides like one inspired. She bends over him. She raises her hands to heaven and speaks!

Numerous as is the throng, they all hear the sound of her voice. Saserna were not better heard.

More marvellous still, they all believe that they understand her command:—

'I charge thee, thou foul spirit, come out of the man and go thy way!'

'The wolf! the wolf! the wolf! See! see! see! The wolf! the wolf!'

The foul spirit has entered the wolf. See! see! the beast, loosed by Simeon, flies, yelling, across the arena, and leaps the iron fence.

Crash! It has leaped headlong into the pit and is dead as a stone.

Meanwhile the fallen man, the possessed, raises himself from the earth on to his knees before Huldah. With reverent, plaintive, scared expression he bends beneath her beatific glance, in mingled sense of love, gratitude, humility, and fear. He seizes the hem of her toga, raises it to his lips and kisses it. He would worship her did she not forbid.

'Not to me, not to me, but to Him in whose name thou art saved from the evil one, be all thy thankfulness and all the glory.'

Strange, strange, oh wondrous strange! he knows the language in which she addresses him. It is like his native tongue.

Dashing his massive club away with his foot and taking her extended hand in his own, he permits her to bring him like a child into the presence of Cæsar. At a sign from her he does humble homage to the mighty leader of the mighty legions, and then, in obedience to an impatient wave of the hand from the Emperor, that he must be instantly removed as a sickening sight, with his head bent on his breast, he suffers himself to be led away by his master Milo along the path by which he entered the theatre.

And the crowd, following him with its thousand eyes, melts, for a moment, into universal sympathy, and heaves its breast with his. So inscrutably subtle is the influence of sympathetic imitation on the human heart.

Of all the spectators of this singular and miraculous scene none are so impressed as Hadrian and Severus. By some secret spring operating on their more refined natures they change in expression: Severus the cold is flushed with red; Hadrian the flushed is awed and even pale. Is this woman, who casts herself again at the Emperor's feet, a goddess? Does she know every imperial secret thought, word, act? Why not? She can cast out a demon! What more marvellous gift? To whom does such a divine being belong, if not to the master of the world ?

There is a cloud on the face of Severus no doubt, but what of that ? Who is Julius Severus when Hadrian wills and fates decree ?

Saserna breaks the spell.

' What is the will of the Emperor towards Simeon the Jew ? '

' Forward ! ' screams the crowd to Simeon. ' Do homage to Cæsar.'

He is brought to the very foot of the throne, and still they cry :

' Do homage to Cæsar ! '

Simeon heeds no word, no request, no prayer, no command.

He faces Cæsar erect, bold, defiant ; and as one greater than he !

CHAPTER VI.

A LIVING TORCH.

EMPEROR and vice-emperor look on the handsome obstinate youth before them with equally strong but widely different sentiments. The Emperor holds him in some kind of admiration and even awe, tempered with a desire to befriend him.

The least submission, and he were the chosen of the chosen of Hadrian.

Severus, keen-sighted, almost guesses the truth. He too has his admiration, but it is admiration mingled with hate approaching to ferocity. Had he supreme command still, not a chance of escape would be open to the already, in his mind, condemned youth.

'Dost thou remember Trajan, noble Severus?' Hadrain asks.

'Oh well, great Prince. Well.'

'In his youth?'

'In his second youth, not his first.'

'Thinkest thou that Simeon resembles him?'

'The resemblance extends to pain now that it is suggested.'

'I remember bringing to Trajan a dispatch from the Senate, and that standing in that posture he was the same though an older man. I remember him as a fellow-villager of Italica, when I, as a boy, saw him as a youth come to the home of his father where I was at play. Then he was actually the same. Can the dead rise, Severus?'

'I see the likeness, Prince: but the people wait!'

'Wert thou ever at the Temple of Daphne? Didst thou ever dip a leaf there, into the fountain of fate?'

'Never, my lord.'

'Didst thou never see the Syrian priestess who ministered in the temple there that was filled with the god?'

'Never.'

'Then hast thou missed a face of beauty and figure of divineness, such as mine eyes have not fallen on since until this hour.'

And, rapt in a reverie which seemed to

him an age, the Emperor is lost to all around except to the youth who stands still so boldly at the foot of his throne.

The murmuring noise of the crowd wakes him from his trance and rouses him to speech.

'If he will not bend to us test him once more by an offering to the gods, to Apollo the Lord of the Sun and Earth.'

The order is forthwith sent out. The priests of Apollo bring a pedestal bearing on each of its sides the image of the Sun and enclosing the mystical emblem to indicate existence or being. They place the pedestal in front of the Emperor. They lay the fuel on the top of the pedestal : they bring the sacred torch and light the fire.

Then they lead the youth Simeon to the side of the pedestal furthest from the throne : they place him with his face to the throne : they bring a small square box containing incense : they open the box, and without violence or wrath bid him take one little pinch and throw it on the fire.

But not a muscle of his rigid frame moves.

The aged officiating priest is moved to tears as the words escape him :—

' The god, my son, whose homage we invoke gives thee light, and heat, and life. At his command the seasons take their course, and night and day are ordained. In his absence thou wert not, nor even he our divine Emperor who longs to save thee.'

Not a muscle of the rigid frame moves.

' By the remembrance of thy father, of the mother that bore thee, of her who may love thee, of thy country, thy people, thyself, obey the command and do homage to the god of gods.'

Not a muscle moves the rigid limbs; but the lips declare in ringing voice :—

'In vain, in vain. I will worship no graven image.'

' Obstinate miscreant ! ' screams Vibullius.

' Brave youth ! ' pronounces Fabius.

' Faithful to death,' whispers Aaron of the Altar. ' Would to God I could die for thee, oh Simeon, son of my people.'

It is impossible to do more in the way of persuasion ; it is impossible now for Hadrian to show mercy.

He consults with Severus, and Saserna is then bidden to take the will of the people.

'Cæsar demands the will of the people.
Is it the will of the people that Simeon the
Jew shall be set free?'

The answer is taken by a movement of
the thumbs.   If the thumbs of a majority of
voters are turned up to the sky, Simeon is
free.   If they are turned down, his fate is
sealed for further sport or torture.

The masses rise, and with one simultaneous
movement extend their open hands and direct
their thumbs to the earth.

Another consultation between Hadrian and
Severus; another message through Saserna.

'Cæsar demands the will of the people for
the sport they desire.'

Many voices are heard, but the one that
prevails carries the day.

'The torch, the torch, the living torch.'

A blast of trumpet proclaims for the first
time the Emperor's will that the general wish
shall be obeyed.   What else can he do?

Let the choicest of Roman soldiers; let
Fidelis himself disobey an imperial command
and who can save him.   Hadrian is two men.

He is man of man, and man of empire. He is the heart of Rome. Stop his beat and the empire may die.

Towards this youth Simeon his natural heart turns while his imperial heart trembles. Intensely impressed at every moment of his life by the sense of the supernatural, he knows not how to act. He is challenged on his very throne, in the face of his army, by a power that sees and reasons. He is moved and challenged by another power hidden in the souls of a stripling boy and an inspired woman. It is like being compressed between the powers of light and darkness; between a sea of solid faces bent on revenge and sport and two shadowy forms, mysterious and fearful, types of the mysterious east, out of which the sun comes forth each morning in his might, always to be born again let man do what he will!

The voice of the people settles the question. It always does.

Seeing the nature of the elements before him, Hadrian knows he must act, for the moment, the common part, let the mystery work, in the end, what it may. He must obey the will of the people.

The trumpet sounds a second time, and Simeon is led to his fate. He is placed at the gateway leading into the small arena. At the gateway is an armed guard ready to cut him to pieces should he attempt escape that way.

Under the eyes of Cæsar he is clothed over his own choice garments with a garment of sackcloth saturated with bitumen; clothed over all his body, his legs and face alone free.

At the third signal, he is to be set on fire from a torch lighted at the pedestal of Apollo and is let loose into the closed ring, there to rave and fight with the flames until he is consumed, or until, in his ungovernable frenzy, he leaps into the pit like the possessed wolf.

The Briton with the scored back makes peace with the centurion who scored him for the news of this ordeal of fire.

'Oh these Romans, how well they understand sport. Wolves first and fire afterwards. The circus knows its own again.' So he taunts his wife, who assents, to his delight, out of fear of him.

Hadrian and Severus once more confer. It would seem that Severus is inclined to object, but is obliged to yield.

Saserna explains aloud.

'It is the will of Cæsar that the path from the outer edge of the pit to the eastern gateway be kept clear, so that the living torch may fly into the country should he escape from the ring. And let no one pursue him.'

The command gives zest to the excitement. It suggests an impossible thing. All the better!

'It affords his gods a better chance of serving him!' says the jesting Vibullius.

'Say rather that it gives him a better chance of serving his God a longer time,' observes Fabius with a respectful reverence that contrasts strongly with the tone of his comrade.

The month in which this tragedy is enacted is September, and the evening is now rapidly closing in. The light is becoming golden red; the clouds are golden, and the atmosphere is filling up with an ether of golden vapour which is as sensible as if it could be sealed up in vases of light and kept for ever.

It is a light that can be felt ; it gives to everything it touches its own hue ; it reaches the
mind as a familiar friend, and fills it with its
own magnetic tone. It is the light of light for
the solemn act about to follow, such a light as
a poor player, could he invent it, would cast
upon his little stage, to colour all, according
to his sense, with the tragic, the majestic,
the sublime. By it, the earth, the trees, the
vast assembly of men and women, the chariots
and horses, the arms, the standards, the
distant hills, the firmament, are made uniform
in colour, and equally beautiful, every defect
concealed in the enrifting glow. Even Simeon
made really hideous, in other light by the
bituminous garb in which he is invested, is
still a handsome statue, a pillar of rough
gold with the face of a god.

Will no one step forth to ask for his
life ?

Will not Fidelis of a hundred years step
forth, and in the name of his own faithful
services, but a few hours ago so loudly ac-
claimed, ask one favour of his lord and master,
the clement Cæsar ?

Alas, such a thought is the last that would

enter his mind. Did Cæsar say to him, 'Fidelis, step forth and fall on thy sword,' he would do it as readily as he would lead out his hundred men to battle.

In the Roman army age does but crystallise obedience.

Will not the woman who has wrought the miracle interpose?

On her the two men, before whom she is reclining, cast their favours. Will she not speak?

She speaks not a word of that kind, but she rises, and picking up her cymbals marches to the side of the condemned man as if preparing to move in triumph with him.

With her cymbals beating time to her voice she sings to him some songs he knows, and to which all they of his race who hear them respond in silent sympathy. The rest merely wonder and listen : they know not the sweet strains nor the assuring words.

The first stanzas are solemn and sorrowful :—

'A people robbed, a people robbed and spoiled !
They are for a prey, and none delivereth : for a spoil,
and none saith, Restore.'

The next are of hope and trust :—

> 'Therefore will I look unto the Lord,
> I will wait for the God of my salvation.
> Rejoice not over me, oh my enemy,
> When I fall I shall rise.'

Quickly the strain changes into one of joy and exultation :—

> 'Thus saith the Lord :
> Fear not, for I have redeemed thee,
> I have called thee by my name, thou art mine.
> When thou passest through the waters I will be with thee
> And through the rivers they shall not overflow thee,
> When thou walkest through the fire thou shalt not be
>   burned.

> 'Fear not, oh Jacob my servant,
> And thou Jeshurun whom I have chosen,
> Fear ye not, neither be afraid.
> I am the Lord, your Holy one, the creator of Israel, your
>   King !

> 'Arise, shine, for thy light is come,
> And the glory of the Lord is upon thee,
> And the Gentiles shall come to thy light
> And kings to the brightness of thy rising :
> Fear ye not, neither be afraid.'

Another blast of the trumpet peals forth and forms a magical ending to the song. The victim is led out to the gateway of the ring.

The torch brought from the altar of the god is applied to the skirts of the bituminous garment, and with a bound the living pillar of fire crosses the arena like a lightning flash; he is seen in the air; he has leapt the palisade and pit at a bound; he is on the pathway towards the open pass; he is through the pass itself and, blazing furiously, is into the valley beyond.

Severus in his rage all but forgets the presence of his Prince. He is about to give an order for pursuit, remembers his place, craves pardon, and, baffled in his design for the moment, falls into silent thought of what shall next be done. The people are maddened with enthusiasm. They are disappointed and yet delighted. A second miracle has been worked for their admiration. Some of them run to the spot to look at the distance the living fire has leaped. Others crowd on the bank of the theatre, and strain their eyes to see the torch still living and flying with the wind.

It descends the steep valley, crosses it, and with dazzling brightness ascends on the other side. It started a pillar of living fire: it narrows into an erect line of fire thinner and

thinner each moment until it is a mere streak
of flame : it becomes a radiant gem, made
more brilliant by the deepening darkness : still
smaller in size, it rises high up on the opposite
ascent it is climbing, until it is a mere speck
of light : it flickers, fades, and vanishes.

The living torch, out of sight, is instantly
out of the mind of that vast assembly. A
man has gone forth from it, a man like
themselves, of flesh and blood the same ; of
sensibilities the same ; of mind and soul the
same.   He has gone forth a sheet of fire!
Does no one ask his fate ?   Does anyone ask
the fate of the deer that over the mountain-
side carries the arrow of the archer in its
vitals?   Does any one ask what is the fate of
a boar that, with maimed limbs from the teeth
of the hounds, has crept into a shelter of wood
and brake where it cannot be further pursued ?
Nonsense!

The gods sent the wretch, man or beast,
for sport, what else?   Some day some one,
climbing the opposite ascent which the living
torch has climbed, may find the charred
remnants of the victim, and kick them over
as those of him who made the wonderful leap.

Good for the future. For the present, that which the crowd wants is more sport, a new pleasure.

Severus has foreseen this desire, and, with clever forecaste, has provided for it. To the sound of many trumpets, and the huzzas of many voices, the Emperor and he have retired in grand procession to the camp, leaving behind them a proclamation of the Emperor's pleasure that the camp shall be illuminated and festivity be the order of the night.

Even to midnight. So ran the proclamation.

᾽ Huzza! Three times three. Huzza! Huzza! Huzza!

CHAPTER VII.

MIRTH AND MYSTERY.

THE Roman soldier knows his duties so well
he always does the same thing in the same
way, and in the best manner.

Whether the order from the superior in
command be to march, to rest, to fight, to
feast, it is carried out instantly. Every man
is ready at every moment.

The order for the festival by night is carried out in this spirit, and the change which
takes place in the camp is the work almost of
magic art. Before Hadrian and Severus have
been an hour in their quarters, a thousand
lamps are mounted on stakes or staves, which
every soldier has in store, and are blazing
away all over the camp and its surroundings.
Other lamps are obtained, and laid on the
ground of the ramparts in holes rapidly cut

to admit the globe of oil, and very soon all the raised structure of the camp can be seen for miles around like a vast mound of fire.

To crown the whole the Pharos or fire-tower in the south-eastern angle of the square is lighted with an enormous pile of dry fuel. The flames of this pile ascend thirty feet above the tower, and light up the whole encampment like a newly risen sun.

Nor is the circus forgotten. It too is soon illuminated, and prepared for dances, feats of strength, and various games in which the ball plays a conspicuous part.

The news of the great festivities flies far and wide the country round, for such a fire was never seen before. Some of the simple country folk think the camp is on fire by accident, but all, like moths, are drawn to it, the knowing ones bringing whatever they possess from which they can earn a fair profit by sale or barter or skilful sport.

Equally rapid are the movements of those who are to be the providers of the temporary feast. The slaves are driven about in all directions, the stores are unpacked, and the kitchen furnaces are hard at work. The men and

women who hang about the camp are allowed
to open their stalls for the sale of wine and oil
and bread. The makers of mirth, the songsters,
the reciters, the mimetic players, the dancers,
the buffoons turn out in their varied costumes.
The musicians gather together in groups, and
tune their stringed instruments for music.
Outside the tents, and along the great highways
and streets of the camp, the tables and reclining
seats or couches are set out, and from the
grand centre the military bands, if they may
be so called, send forth their stimulating
strains of melody.

Within two short hours the whole of the
populace of this Roman centre of life, usually
so staid, mechanical, and solemn, is one vast
orgie, controlled easily if troublesome, but in
due bounds left to itself to do and work its
own will and pleasure.

It is indeed a picturesque and curious scene
in which we now take part.

For sixty miles around the Pharos sends
forth its sunlike rays, and signals from it fly
to tell to neighbouring camps the special
honour that belongs to ours.

The main street of our camp, which divides

the tents or huts of the common soldiers from the quarters of the officers, is specially attractive, not only for its feastings, but for its transformation into quite a fairy-land. The forum in the centre of this street, in which, when required, the Prætor sits in judgment, is turned into a theatre, from the stage of which those who are gifted with eloquence of speech or song are called forth, imperatively, to display their powers for the common merriment. Some are called to deliver verses and legends from the great Roman writers or poets ; some, natives of Britain, are brought out to dance ; some, conjurers, are made to conjure and cast fortunes ; some, athletes, are made to perform feats of strength or agility.

As the night advances, and the stock of amusements around the grand centre begins rather to flag, there is a cry for Tinnius the Red beard. What he is to do no one knows or cares to enquire, for he is a favourite who always does something new and pleasing, and at all costs he, therefore, must be had and heard.

The cry is loud for Tinnius Rufus the Red-beard, and when, very much worried by his virago, who sticks to him like a limpet, he makes his way through the crowd to gain the tribune, the cheering, which extends from one end of the camp to the other, tells the Emperor and Severus, as they talk together after the Emperor has partaken alone of his simple evening meal, a crust of bread with fruit, a few sweet herbs, and a flask of vinegar wine, that something specially entertaining is about to occur.

'What,' asks the Emperor of an attendant, 'what does this ringing uproar mean?'

The attendant, a bashful youth, answers: 'Tinnius Rufus, Prince, the Red beard, is about to sing from the Forum.'

For a moment all is quiet to the ears of the distinguished rulers, but soon, ten times louder than ever, the applause is resumed.

'Tinnius the Red-beard, great Prince, is called upon to sing again.'

Tinnius, in short, has got an enthusiastic and obstinate encore, an encore so enthusiastic and so obstinate it moves the Emperor himself to go and share with the audience in the fun which has been elicited.

The thing is easily done: that plain soldier

may go, under the artificial light, wherever he lists and not be known. Severus must remain, Hadrian may go.

Wending his way through the crowd quite unrecognised, Hadrian soon attains what he wants—a quiet place near the Forum where he can see and not be conspicuously seen.

The great Tinnius is still receiving the plaudits of his admirers. The great man bows to his admirers, just as great men always bow. The admirers renew the cheer, and then call silence for the great man.

Tinnius advances in correct fashion to face his audience. Clothed in mock imperial robes, he stands under a little bower of lamps; he draws from his bosom a scroll at which he glances furtively. Then he clears his throat, and, taking his key from the twang of a lute, he sings out again, in a voice which supplies in power whatever it wants in sweetness, the song that has been so loudly encored. It is a song intended for the occasion, an impromptu very difficult to be understood by the native part of the audience, but to the Roman part, dry and spry and sly.

THE SONG OF TINNIUS RUFUS THE RED-BEARD.

Ecce Imperator !

Jupiter from heaven glancing
Fix'd his godlike eyes on earth.
Soldiers singing, maidens dancing
Filled him full of jealous mirth.
Maidens dancing, soldiers singing
Not of him the great creator,
But in raptest chorus ringing,
         Ecce Imperator !

All the gods unto him calling,
' See,' he cried, ' yon mortal, see !
Thousand slaves around him falling
Worship him instead of me.
Next with rebel voice appalling
They will name him our dictator.
We must stop their wanton brawling,
         Ecce Imperator !

Hercules ! with club descending,
Dash him from his mocking throne.
Mercury ! thy bright bow bending,
Send a shaft through flesh and bone.
Esculapius ! poisons blending,
Be our arch administrator,
Stop their wretched throats from rending,
         Ecce Imperator ! '

Quick as thought the gods, obeying
Their august and mighty lord,
Hastened to prepare for slaying
Him the mortal hosts adored.

But the goddesses, arraying
All their forces for the traitor,
Echoed what the men were saying,
    Ecce Imperator !

Vanquished Jove to Cæsar bowing
Stands a mark for gods and men,
Day and night for ever showing
Powers of gods and men are vain,
With the goddesses bestowing
On their choice their imprimatur ;
Name and fame and love endowing :
    Ecce Imperator!

Romans ! to your Tinnius bringing
All your love and loyalty.
While the goddesses are flinging
Him their smiles and kisses sly ;
Let your powerful voices ringing
Tell the gods that no one greater,
Could be found to hear you singing,
    Ecce Imperator!

The effect of the refrain of this song throughout the camp is like a whirlwind. Tinnius sang the song, but Saserna, the 'editor,' or master of ceremonies, wrote it, and, being a true lover of the anonymous, is not a little proud of his performance. There is a pride in the anonymous greater often than in the nonymous, and Saserna feels it keenly. Very shrewdly, he has placed himself not many yards from the quarters of Hadrian, and, as his voice of thunder takes up the refrain, the whole camp follows his lead so completely that it were dangerous for any one to be silent.

The situation held, at the moment, by the Emperor, proud as it may seem to be, is not without its embarrassments ; for he, ranking as a common soldier, dare do no more nor less than join in voice loyally with the rest.

An Emperor may be troubled when he hears himself made, by the tongue of the joker, a mark for public comment ; and as the droll Tinnius rolled out and emphasised, with gestures that cannot be written down, the allusions to the goddesses, a thought pricks the imperial mind that perhaps a satire deep and sore, for which, as we may see later on, there is some loose foundation, is conveyed. But when the merry songster, in the final verse, assumes all the glory to himself, and, with infinite humour of manner and assumption of imperial dignity, claims to himself the smiles and kisses of the goddesses, and the adoration of the people, the perfect innocency of any insult withdraws the suspicion, and sends the Imperator back to his tent one of the chief laughers of the whole laughing encampment; while the Red-beard, released from his temporary dignity, becomes the hero of the hour, and ' Ecce Imperator ' the facile password to all good fellowship.

How many flagons of Roman wine and of British mead are drunken to-night to ' Ecce Imperator,' it would be as hard as sad to tell ; for all except the Emperor are slaves to wine at festive times. He, with the stern simplicity of a Stoic, returns to his tent unattended. Severus has prudently retired to his own quarters, duties, or pleasures, and the Emperor is left all alone according to his imperial will.

A plainer tent than the imperial tent no travelling officer or soldier in the whole army could possess. In five minutes of time it can be struck or set in full form ready for his use and occupation. When he is out of it, inspecting troops, making surveys, delivering judgments, presiding over councils, or planning fortifications—and he would often take part in all these things in the course of a single day—the soldiers get sly peeps, at all risks, into this marvellous tent. To be caught within it might, under strict rule, mean condign punishment, but no one ever suffers for his curiosity. In point of fact, Hadrian rather enjoys the inquisitiveness, and allows it tacitly to work out his own ends. There is nothing in the tent to conceal, and the simplicity of it is an example of order and power. If he, the master of all the legions, can be satisfied with so simple an apartment, by what right can an idle patrician claim more of luxury, and of what have the common soldiers to complain?

In an empire of soldiers no example were wiser or stronger. The tent itself is of the usual round and pointed form ; but at each side there runs off from it a little pavilion, holding a bed or couch raised but a foot or so from the earth. In the centre of the tent is a small table with a reclining couch aside it. Upon the table is a book, a Roman translation of the works of the learned Jew, Josephus, who had fought and written during the wars of his people under Vespasian and Titus, an hour-glass, and a lighted candle. The candle is peculiar. It indicates the time from hour to hour. It is made of wax, coloured in sections, each section marked with a Roman numeral, and each having the capacity of burning one hour, a primitive silent candle-clock, which always burns and records time in that tent when the sun has gone to rest. By this primitive time-piece, invented by the Emperor himself, he knows that it is within an hour of midnight, an hour later than usual for bed.

His young attendant has by his order joined the sports, so he waits on himself.

He takes off his accoutrements, lays his sword on the table, passes into his sleeping pavilion, returns invested in a warm purple robe or dressing-gown, his sole garment of imperial quality, sits down on the couch, and, bringing the candle near to him, commences listlessly to read the book before him.

It is in vain ! He cannot read, he cannot sleep according to his usual custom, for he is vexed, perplexed, and anxious. He is vexed that one of his mandates has not been obeyed. He told Severus that he wished to converse with the remarkable stranger and child whom he had discovered in the crowd at the time of the combat, and he has learned, at his frugal supper, that the two have mysteriously disappeared, just before the scene of the flying torch, and can nowhere be found. No one saw these illustrious strangers come, no one saw them depart. They had neither eaten, drunken, nor spoken with living soul. Their costume alone had suggested to Severus that they had come from the western Isle of Peace and Beauty. Musing on this circumstance, the mind of the Emperor wanders to that stiff-necked youth, who, as if he were a king over death himself, had refused, him, Hadrian, the ruler of all the world, the meanest reverence.

Never before has mortal man dared to treat the Cæsar in such a manner.

The insult stings; but this diversion of his thoughts subsides in the remembrance of the maiden of magic and grace, who reclined at his feet, who cast out the evil spirit from that monster of a man, and who sang the strange songs to the youth about to die.

Of these divinely endowed creatures he has heard, and doubts not they exist. His mind goes back once more to the sacred Temple where there was such a woman whom the priests of the temple retained as a Syrian or Jewish prophetess, and whom Trajan loved and perhaps bore away.

Gifts like these are, like features, inherited. Could this woman be her child?

No, her face is neither the face of Trajan nor of the Jewess: were it the face of that rebellious youth the suspicion would be true. or might be true, at least. Straining to recall many long-forgotten details he returns, in thought, to the man and the child, in their mantles of emerald green. They have no real voice, and yet they seem to say to him: 'Hold that woman in thy safe keeping; let her never depart from thy power, for she is thy incarnate, thy good spirit.'

It was one of those brief deliriums in which recent events wake up some of the drowsy senses to future life and action. But these deliriums are potent ministries. They have made more real history than all the hosts of real men who ever took the field. They are an ordination of supreme nature herself directing events. They are the soul of the supernatural, and yet are the commonest humanity. They have given birth to faiths, religions, wars, crusades, revolutions, empires.

And now once more they play their part.

The first man of Rome, rising up to his full intelligence from one of these deliriums, accepts the manifestation, and declaring 'It shall be done,' sinks on his couch into deep and long repose.

Cæsar sleeps! A goddess in the form of a god rises amongst men!

CHAPTER VIII.

LAID LOW WITH WINE.

WHILST the master of the legions takes his repose the camp is still awake. There is yet plenty of time · left for continuance of the revelry, and, although the native part of the population, and they who live outside the camp, are fast dissolving, so as to reach their various homes, the Roman soldiers remain in festivity. They have ceased to sing and to dance, but they are little less merry, for they recline around the festive tables either within or at the doors of their tents or huts, tell stories of the past, discuss current topics, praise women and wine, and laugh and joke as Roman soldiers off duty always do.

But they are ready at a moment's call for duty when that is required.

'They always come when I call them, and sometimes they come when I don't call them.'

That was the slow and only joke of Fidelis, the centurion of a hundred years; a joke calculated to become lasting as time.

Together with the soldiers, the officers, from the centurions upwards, have also their enjoyments. In their various quarters they form their little coteries, and, marching out at various intervals to witness the outside amusements, return to their wine and their private merriment.

Of the groups of officers and friends which lend themselves to the general and private mirth one is of special interest to us.

It is in the quarters of Tinnius Rufus. It is made up of that worthy himself, of the two new arrivals, Fabius and Vibullius, and of Saserna, 'the editor,' as he is called, of the ceremonies, and the director of the Mappa at the sport that has been carried out during the previous day.

These men were all old companions in Rome, as schoolfellows in their young days, and although they were of somewhat different rank, station and fortune, they continue attached friends, and rejoice much at meeting together once again.

Fabius is one of the choicest living representatives of patrician Rome. In the early and troublous times, ere yet the plebeians had any power, the ancestors of Fabius were conspicuous not only for their greatness but for their liberality. They fought for the honest privileges of the plebs, and did much for securing the same. They stood by the measure which gave the lower grades their power, and they and their descendants were beloved and respected of all men. At the same time no patricians were more enamoured of their own dignity. They laboured for the people, but they kept their own; perhaps, if the truth were told, their method was nothing more than pride feeding on craft.

Our Fabius has the rich blood of his ancestors in his veins, and his veins are overflowing.

Vibullius is patrician also, but of different stamp. Under the first Cæsar, one of his ancestors by his skill and bravery attained to knightly rank and was much esteemed. Amongst other gifts he possessed that of imitation, and in private life often amused his friends by his perfect mimicries. The gift, unfortunately, became known to the Dictator, who straightway commanded him to play some small mimetic piece publicly in his presence. The Dictator must be obeyed, but the obedience of the noble knight was at a sacrifice which Cæsar himself could not restore. To play a part as a public player was a duty too ignoble, even under command, to be allowed to pass amongst the patricians. In humiliation the injured man practically left Rome and Roman society, and, as a favour, obtained permission from Octavius, the second of the Cæsars and the first Emperor, to take the name of Vibullius for his original family name of Ambivius. His son, who inherited great wealth, owing to the accumulation of wealth during his father's enforced retirement, became a man designated as one of 'softened pleasures with penurious failings,' and from him the race was continued in much the same condition. Our Vibullius is of this cast. He is courted for his wealth more than his rank; he is trusted because he takes care of what he has; and he is liked because, whilst he enjoys himself, he diffuses a charm of good nature, which seems reckless but is really under perfect control, round all

with whom he mixes. He and Fabius agree,
notwithstanding their differences of mind and
nature. Fabius is learned, classical, liberal,
philosophic, proud. Vibullius is little learned,
is no classic, is an aristocrat in feeling, a tyrant
at heart in regard to the people, flippant in
mode of thought and expression, vain rather
than proud, but good-natured, like Fabius, and
very good company.

Both, as far as possible, have avoided arms
as a profession. They have got substitutes
whenever they could find them, and the find
under the magic of money has been easily conceived and brought forth.

Saserna, the editor or master of the
ceremonies, is a cousin of Fabius by his
mother's side. His mother, with a woman's
weakness, must needs form a romantic attach-
ment in her early life with a Hercules named
Saserna, who played a somewhat conspicuous
part in the court of Domitian, and who was
accredited, not without favour from the people,
with having aided Domitia and Parthenius in
their successful plot against that Emperor's life,
by coming in as a gladiator to assist Stephanus,
the comptroller of the household, in his fatal

attack on the hated tyrant. This Saserna, under the reign of Trajan, rose into position with that monarch, took the editorship of his ceremonial affairs with great skill, and dying at a full age left a son, our Saserna, who, possessing many of his father's qualities, is now editor to Julius Severus in Britain.

The last man of our group, Tinnius Rufus Vigilius, whom we already know by sight and name and voice, is, like· Saserna, of broken descent, but is admitted into the charmed circle of the empire. His uncle, Vigilius Rufus, had been the colleague of the short-lived and gentle Emperor Nerva, the successor of Domitian and predecessor of Trajan, and had even opposed Nerva for the crown. Forgiven by Nerva, Vigilius still hoped for the succession ; but Nerva left it to Trajan, who, promptly, sent the whole family, root and branch, as exiles to Britain, where they worked for their bread as best they could. Our man, witty, ready, good-hearted, and possessed of the rare art of writing well, has become scribe and comptroller to Severus, and, known, by name at least, in every British·Roman camp, is a universal favourite, a hail-fellow-well-met sort of being, greeted everywhere, as one who, in jest, can say and sing, safely, things which, said or sung in jest or earnest by another, might easily cost that other his head. He is always called Tinnius Rufus by his friends because of his sounding jollity, his family name of Vigilius being now almost forgotten.

'Ecce Imperator!' exclaims Vibullius, as Tinnius enters his tent to rejoin his comrades after he has delivered to the mob his now famous song. 'Ecce Imperator!' bursts out the rolling voice of Saserna. 'Thou didst thy part, my Tinnius, like an Emperor. Had Vigilius thy uncle been as acute as his name made him out to be, thou his heir might have worn the real instead of the sham purple to-night.'

Reclining on their couches, the four friends sip their wine, and talk over the events of the day with such absorption that the trumpet-call at midnight for the camp to close comes upon them with a start.

They rise to the call, and go forth to see the end of the eventful day.

The rapidity with which the camp is closed is a phenomenon. Every man doing his work always in the same way, and that way always the best, the whole encampment at once is transformed; the streets are cleared; the lamps are extinguished, at a sign, simultaneously; and under the fading fire of the Pharos the sentinels are performing their guardianship as if no feast had ever been held.

'Give me a Roman army as a time-keeper and I will challenge Phœbus himself to keep better time,' observes Fabius, with true admiration of what he has witnessed.

But hark! What noise is there, disturbing the dead silence which for a brief interval prevails?

Quickly a troop of horsemen, fifty at least, passes by, headed by an officer of well-known skill. The troop makes for the southern gateway, and like a stone from a catapult is out of the fortress.

'What new freak is this?' enquires the hasty Vibullius.

Saserna and Tinnius may both know, but if they do they are not ready to tell.

Saserna answers off hand as if it were, as indeed to him it is, a trifling episode :—

'A despatch, perchance, from the Emperor

or Severus to another camp ; or a scouting party to watch some wretched native force that is threatening to rise.'

It matters not, the troop is gone, and the friends, who, by their position and rank, are privileged to continue their pleasure, resume their places and their discourse. They resume the subject of their meeting during the sports of the previous day.

'I saw you both enter the popularia,' observed Saserna, ' and but for the presence of Severus the watchful, I should have made you some sign of recognition.'

'Is Severus still the severe ?' asks Vibullius.

'Unchanged and unchangeable. As stern in the camp as when he was prefect in the academy and we four boys were under his dominion. Tinnius is always repeating what you have just hinted, Vibullius, that his name carries his nature. Does he ever slacken, Tinnius you sly old cannibal, under that wine of Cyprus you so freely supply him with ?'

'As Hercules slackens under his club, great editor. Wine makes Severus more severe, until he suddenly sinks dead under it alto- gether, a log of a man.'

' Does he never, when you two are alone, speak of the past?' enquired Fabius. 'Our parents were all of equal blood with his and we with him.'

'With the side blood of the illustrious Virgil flowing in your veins, distinguished Fabius. But I can tell you he never speaks except on business, in which he is as sharp as a sword-point, as hard as an executioner.'

' Will the ass know us when he meets us, Tinnius?' interposed Vibullius.

'The ass will not know you, for he is a dumb ass, and a blind ass, and a deaf ass to all except his own business, and that is Severus himself. He, I am sure, recognised you to-day. The Emperor in his place would have sent for you, and in the presence of all the people would have folded you in his embrace. He, true to himself, sat like a stone and stared like a statue. Perchance to-morrow he will ask me what you do here, and if he thinks that you mean to stay he will offer you some office about his person, for he has a strange liking to have around him those he knows and trusts. Beyond that not a syllable.'

' What did he to the Emperor, Saserna?'

'The same, my Fabius, as to us all, his
duty, his bare duty. Yet I noticed that
Hadrian touched him once in a vital point,
though it was by a mere arrow shot at a venture.'

'About what?' all the friends eagerly wish
to know.

'The dark maiden who laid herself like a
beautiful sleuthhound at Hadrian's feet.'

'The sorceress who went round with old
hundred years, and cast out the demon, and
sang the gibberish to the boy Simeon as he
started for the lower gods,' put in Tinnius.
'But my friends you have no wine,' and so
saying he refilled their cups that they might
listen, with their greedy ears, more keenly to
Saserna for the vital point that had been
touched in Severus the severe.

'It caught my ear. The Emperor asked
him who the maiden was, and after getting
his reply twitted him with being in love. And
mark you, my brothers, for once and for the
only time in my life I saw Severus wince.'

'Antony and Cleopatra re-enacted,' exclaims Tinnius. 'We will put it into a play,
most potent editor, with your assistance. He

shall be Antony, the beautiful sorceress shall be Cleopatra. By Minerva 'twill be the root of a new poem.'

'And why not?' suggests Fabius. 'Why not, you excited red-beard. What is there strange that is not familiar in love? Every Cleopatra has an Antony.'

'Two or three,' interposed Tinnius.

'Well, two or three, three or four, four or five, if you like; it is by the will of the gods.'

'I should say the goddesses,' again interrupted the vivacious scribe; 'I should say by the order of the goddesses, my noble Roman.'

'By the goddesses then, if you will; still there is in the fact no wonder.'

'No wonder,' retorts Tinnius. 'No wonder! Why, I tell you,' and here he struck the wine table a blow which stung his own hand as he poured out his emphatic sentence, 'I tell you I would as soon expect to see Julius Severus lift up the curtains of this tent and walk in here and take that empty couch as believe that he should ever light on a Cleopatra.'

The words are scarcely said, the wine cups have not ceased to ring on the vibrating table

when the curtain rises and, to the blank
astonishment of them all, the face and form of
Severus is before them.

He is divested now of all robes and marks
of office. Attired in the simple evening robe
of the Roman gentleman, erect as a pillar
and hard as marble, he stands before them;
his features finely chiselled in every line and
more rigid than his body.

A man by nature commanding, and from
his cradle a Roman soldier intended for command, the form and manner and will of the
soldier is in every look and movement evolved
through generations of his kind. His ancestors
had never been of his own rank, but from
father to son they had been centurions, until
they became so by natural birthright and
claimed their own with unswerving zeal and
confidence. In the days of Julius Cæsar,
Labienus, one of the family, having proved
himself an admirable shipbuilder by rapidly
reconstructing at Dola a battered squadron
that had conveyed Cæsar from Gaul, was left
in Britain, with a higher command, to pene-
trate far westward into the island, and con-
quer along his way until he met the sea on

the western side. He did it, and the work was done so well that superior rank was awarded to him and Julius was added to his name.

It was, however, reserved for the man who stands now before us to make the most notable mark in arms and name, and to achieve a position, viceregal in quality, as governor of the province which his ancestor had fought and overcome. Detailed, in the early part of his career, to hold with two hundred men a strong fortalice of stone while his general in command went out with the main body of the troops to find and vanquish a formidable native force that had collected in Siluria, he was so suddenly surrounded by an overwhelming body of the enemy that escape and defence seemed equally impossible. Three parts out of four of his fortress were invested, the fourth part not immediately in danger being a lofty hill which formed the back of his quarry.

In an hour his plan of action was matured, and the order went forth as the night shut off the foe and checked the complete investment. 'Let one hundred men cut through that hill a tunnel of sufficient size for one man to pass; but conceal the escape on the opposite side.

Let the rest destroy every roof and wall within the fortress that might afford covering or shelter.'

By the following morning's dawn the tunnel was complete. Then, giving orders that every man should be ready to obey his word to enter the tunnel and pass out of it in line, he himself mounting the gateway of the fortress signalled to the enemy to bring them within call.

Assuming the rôle of a young and alarmed sentinel who had been coerced into the army, and speaking to the ambassadors in their own language, which he had completely mastered. he offered to admit them all at the gate while his comrades still slept, if they would let him, without any weapon, run, afterwards, for his life.

The bait took ; the native force was drawn as quickly as possible towards the gate of the little fortress, and so soon as the assumed sentinel had got his men ready for their exit by the tunnel and on their way to it, he himself throwing open the gate escaped as promised into the rear of the enemy.

The witless host swept in slowly through

the narrow gateway, to find not one lance or
sword to oppose them. In momentary triumph
they wondered what had happened. But they
only waited for their doom.

'A cave! a cave!' they cried, 'the Romans
have hidden in a cave!'

Impetuously they enter, and some of them
creep along the floor of the cave until in
darkness they try to turn back to tell that
there seems no enemy there, except darkness
and suffocating air. The check created a
panic, and a resolve of the enemy to return
to the open plain.

It was too late. The besiegers were the
besieged. By the time they had discovered
the trick that had been played on them fifty
Roman soldiers were at the outer portal slaying instantly every man who tried to escape
through its narrow space, while a small body
of sappers at the free end of the tunnel
closed that so strongly with earth that no
vent was there. Locked in the strongly built
prison with no means to scale its bare and
lofty walls, with no means to concentrate
more than ten men at most at the portal,
against a drilled troop on the other side, they

soon found themselves stoned from the slings of the Romans with such vehemence that they were enveloped in a shower of missiles falling from tremendous heights like massive hail-stones, from which there was no shelter, and which wounded and killed all on whom they fell. In the panic they closed on each other, and soon the Roman swordsmen boldly re-entering the gate finished the deadly work which the slingers had commenced.

The helplessly terrified victims who re-mained prayed for mercy. They prayed in vain. Severus, who had himself slain a little hecatomb, commanded that two only should live, the two men with whom he had par-leyed and who had promised him his liberty and his life, and these were led forth, not out of any pity or care for their lives, but that they might run and tell to their people how a new Roman general had risen whose skill was equal to his cruelty and his courageous craft.

Henceforth the Roman strategist, so cun-ning and so merciless, was made to assume a new name, which attached itself to him until he was bound to accept it whether he liked it or not. It suited his nature to its very core to like and adopt the name, and from that day Julius Labienus was known by all men as Julius Severus.

The news of his stratagem reached Rome, and was hailed there as a triumphant achievement. This was good for Severus. The news of the stratagem penetrated everywhere through the native tribes of Britain, and that was good for Rome. So far from bearing enmity to the man for what he had done, the native enemy revered his cunning and his courage. It struck them with an admiring fear, and made Julius Severus himself worth a legion to the Roman arms. The place where his victory was won he converted into a tumulus called 'the cave of the slain,' or sometimes the tomb by Severus.

Upon the mind of Marcus ~~Aurelius~~ who was Emperor when this event occurred, the victory of Severus told badly. But Trajan, who soon afterwards succeeded, was very differently influenced. This fighting prince saw in Severus a soldier who knew his own mind and carried out his own desires with the mercilessness of fate, a man of men for subduing and ruling savage hordes. So, under

Trajan, Severus found ample scope for his skill and food for his ambition. Kept in command of one of the most remote of the Roman possessions, he was safe from disturbing the ruling power at home; while in his own sphere he was, in every practical sense, an Emperor. He knew his place, kept it, and made it respected and feared by the exercise of the severest will blended with the severest justice.

Until civilisation breeds and nourishes philanthropy as the light of the world, such men as Julius Severus always rule best, and on the whole, perhaps, most humanely. They rule through perfect fear, and, until perfect love casteth out fear, they will never be deposed.

We see this man now before us more closely than when he sat in the seat of state of the Circus Britannicus. He is forty years old. He is at this moment effecting a new and startling strategy, and we who have the privilege to know his secret may tell it. He comes ostensibly to greet in an informal way his two old schoolfellows, whom he has detected as fresh from Rome. He comes actually to hear from them in their accidental gossipings the state of Rome and the position of Hadrian in the minds of the Roman people. Severus is in his prime as a soldier; Hadrian somewhat past his prime, is not a soldier. Is the empire falling to pieces, disintegrating, under a more benign but less conquering power than existed during Trajan's brief but glorious rule?

In plain thoughts, has Julius Severus any chance for the imperial purple?

A Roman less severe than he, though holding higher dignity, on entering into the company of two old friends whom he has not seen for many years, would greet them with the kiss of friendship, would enquire after their health, their home, their family, their friends.

With Severus no such kindly ceremony is either expected or offered.

In the quarters of every superior person in the Roman camp there is provided a chair or couch of state, called emphatically the ' empty couch.' It is reserved exclusively for the father of the people, for him who governs, just as in a private house the couch or seat of the father of the house is retained for him alone.

In these quarters of Tinnius Rufus the comptroller the seat of honour is of course there, and though it has never been filled it is always brought forth. Symbolically the sire or ruler is always at the feast, be it ever so rich, ever so homely.

To that seat with all the dignity of his office Severus moves, and takes it without a word; the head and master of the school-boy group once more.

The wine continues to pass, and gradually amongst the old friends a warm but less animated conversation ensues, to which Severus listens, but in which, except by a nod or a word or two like Yes and No, he takes no part. But, in one respect he more than joins the rest.

The wine with which the liberal comp-troller freely supplies him suits his palate, and of it he drinks with a kind of savage greed, until at length, after a larger draught than ordinary, his hard features become imbecile, his head drops on his chest, and he falls, as the comptroller said, like Hercules on his club, a helpless log of human flesh and bone.

' He is off,' observes Tinnius, ' so dead off

that we might if we liked put him through
the fire and into his urn, and he be none the
wiser.'

'It was our conversation about the Jewish
sorceress which made him expedite this
quotidian fit by that copious finishing draught,'
remarks Saserna.

And therewith follows a consultation as to
what is to be done.

'We must bear him gently and quietly to
his quarters,' explains Tinnius. 'In eight
hours he will be the same Severus as he was
in the tribune, with a little more of the demon
mocking him into severity.'

Practised hands in all works connected
with the camp, the friends, in a few moments,
fit up an ambulance or litter from the spears
which stand around. They lash the spears
together into the litter, cover it with the skin
of a leopard which lies over the back of one
of the couches, then folding the body of the
vice-emperor in the folds, with a cushion for his
head, Fabius and Vibullius hoist him on their
shoulders, and following Tinnius and followed
by Saserna move rapidly and noiselessly
towards their destination.

By this time all the camp is at rest except the sentinels, who keep up their unwearied watch, and who are doubly strong at the quarters where slaves and foreigners reside.

The stars alone give light, the winds alone give motion.

The bearers of Severus traverse almost the entire length of the central street of the camp. They pass the silent tent of the Emperor, around which the sentinels stand, like statues, in absolute rest. They pass the tent of the physician of the Emperor, the learned Asclepias Tryphonius, usually called Tryphon. They pass the newly erected and singular tents of the various scholars, engineers, and mechanics, who invariably accompany the Emperor wherever he goes, and in whose discourse he finds his chief delight.

As they approach the quarters of Severus, which lie outside the encampment, in more permanent structure than any in the rest of the camp—a Roman villa in point of fact—they observe in one tent a single light and some sign of movement within. It is the only tent that has given the faintest indication of the life that nestles in its walls.

It is the tent of Fidelis the centurion of a hundred years.

Fabius and Vibullius, anxious to complete their task, step after Tinnius rapidly. Saserna follows, but having less cause for hurry waits for a moment. His curiosity, always keen, is awakened by the light and the movement in the old man's quarters, and as he approaches them he draws himself near to the entrance wondering what is going on within.

As he waits the canvas doors of the tent open, and there steps quietly out into the night a stranger whom, from his garb, a long flowing dark robe, he, with some hesitation, at last decides to be the Archiater or Emperor's physician, the renowned Tryphon.

Saluting so great a person with deep reverence, the editor enquires, with becoming respect, whether anything has befallen Fidelis that has called for the skill of the physician.

'I came,' replies Tryphon, 'as one searching for all knowledge of hidden things. I came to the tent of Fidelis the centurion, to see with my own eyes, to listen with my own ears, and to touch with my own hands, one who has lived a hundred years. I wished to feel the pulses of so strange a man; but above all I desired to learn from his lips by what art he had attained to such an enduring life.'

' A noble research, most learned Tryphon, if I may venture to call thee, so much my senior, by thy familiar name.'

' 'Tis the name I most love, my son,' responds the Archiater, ' for 'tis the name my good parents left me, and 'twas their great wealth. But speaking of this task of mine thou dost overrate its worth. The physician has two duties ever on his hands: the one to the sick man who is under his care, the other to the world at large over which also his skill ranges. It is his duty, as the wisest man of my people teaches, to seek and know all things that happen under the sun : this sore travail hath God given to the sons of men to be exercised therewith.'

' A noble duty nobly expounded, Tryphon. No wonder is it that thy imperial master keeps thee as the apple of his eye ; but pray tell me of this old centurion, what thinkest thou of him?'

' A wonderful remnant of a human soul and body, Saserna, for thy voice carries thy name ; a wonderful remnant of a human soul in human form, of whom let me speak to thee in parable. Dost thou remember near to Rome a lofty pedestal at the foot of the Aventine hills?'

'I remember it well; it was raised by our great fathers of the state to the goddess of health, Salus, and it stood there for ages defying time.'

'It did, but now knowest thou its fate?'

'Not more than I have told you, illustrious healer!'

'Then I will tell you more. One morning, a month or so ere we left Rome for this remote island, that statue stood in all its apparent strength and in all its beauty. It was the day of the festival dedicated to the goddess, and in honour of the event a smart and handsome youth was chosen to climb the statue and place a garland on her brow. A hundred times before the same ceremony had been performed; again the rite was fully carried out, and again at night the sun cast his parting rays on the garlanded Salus. But in the night there rose a storm, and when the sun threw his glory once more on the charmed spot the statue of Salus lay as dust at the foot of its crumbling pedestal, the garland buried in the ruins.'

'Alas! alas! And is that the fate of Fidelis?'

'It is. The light crown which Severus put on the old man's head yesterday has borne him to the earth.'

'Dead?' exclaimed Saserna.

'No, not dead, but in his last hours; a centurion still: yet in the bonds of death and past my art to save.'

'Will he live long?'

'Not to see the full glory of the day, Saserna. When the symbol of your Roman god Apollo, the symbol of his everlasting existence, his *yes*, his great *I am*, the eternal sun, is longest away from the earth the feeble of the sons of men, though they were once the strongest, depart before the breath of his rising and are no more. Farewell!'

And gathering up his robe the Archiater turns back from Saserna to seek his own place by the side of the Cæsar he so faithfully serves.

For a brief period Saserna, wholly absorbed in the parable he has heard, stands at the door of Fidelis. He would enter had he not been arrested by the gentle voice of Huldah, who seems to him to commence singing to the God of her faith a prayer she has turned into the Latin tongue to make it more familiar to the dying Roman.

> ' Wait ! wait ! for the Lord ;
> Let thy soul wait for the Lord,
> And trust thou in His word.
> Wait thou for the Lord
> More than the watchers wait
> Who look out for the dawn,
> For the dawn, for the dawn of day.'

'It is as if she were singing a babe to its sleep with her foot upon its cradle,' muses the editor ; 'and so she sings that infant of a hundred years to his eternal rest. But to which of the immortal gods she chants I trow not. Jove is not chaste enough, Mars is too savage. It must be to the God of her own people to whom was built the gorgeous temple which Vespasian laid in ruins, with the city called Jerusalem in which it stood, and near to which Fidelis was born.'

And, continuing his musing but not daring to break the divine song, Saserna, with the words still on his ear :—

' Wait ! wait ! for the Lord ;
Let thy soul wait for the Lord,
And trust thou in His word,'

follows rapidly his friends to the villa of Severus.

He passes through a passage in the pine wood, reaches the threshold of the residence and, after lighting his lamp quickly with flint and steel, enters the first court in which persons who come on business are received. Crossing this he ascends by two steps to the middle court, where favoured guests are permitted to enter. Thence he passes into a third court, on the right of which is the sleeping room of the man laid low with wine, and treading noiselessly joins his comrades there, to give them, if need be, any assistance they may require.

The house, or as it is commonly called the Court of Severus, is the type of the Roman dwelling, like that in which Sallust lived in his day, but changed a little to suit the variable and sometimes severe climate of Britain. It is built within the ever-green pine wood, the branches of which both shelter and purify it. It is furnished to suit not so much the taste as

the service of its master. It is literally filled
with the various requirements of the soldier:
armour, arms, movable folding tents, and
everything that is portable and useful in the
field. The middle part, used for the reception of visitors by most Romans, is here a
museum and library. Its walls are covered
with maps of the country, of towns, rivers,
plains, roads and harbours. It is Britain con-
densed to the eyes of its master; whilst its
floor is strewn with trophies and relics of various
campaigns, ranged in order, but not in such
order that a stranger would understand them.
Adjoining the room in which the now helpless
warrior sleeps, the sleep of wine, is the hot-air
or Roman bath, in which the people of Rome,
losing by this time their rude strength, are
beginning to indulge with too wanton indul-
gence. Each Roman who can afford it has
now his hot-air bath. the Emperor excepted,
and Severus following the custom has his in
his own house. To him the bath is a saving
remedy. In it he evaporates off into the air
the fumes of the one and only enemy that
even laid him low.

Ere Saserna arrives the friends have re-

moved the insensible Severus from the ambulance, 'have skinned the leopard,' as Tinnius
profanely remarks, and have laid him on his
own couch as dense a log as ever.

'Take care,' continues Tinnius, ' take care
that you move nothing to show you have
entered his sepulchre, and carry away carefully the skin and the spears. He will wake
up then, thinking he got home of his own will
and strength.'

They follow the injunction to the letter :
leave in his degraded glory the leader of
Roman Britain to fight his most fatal foe ;
and return to the home of Tinnius just as
the day is beginning to dawn.

CHAPTER IX.

INTERPOSITION.

WE see by the history of the last chapter how some favoured ones of the Roman camp ended the festivity of the preceding day. But there are others under our care, and one especially whose course and fate must claim our close and immediate attention.

The masses went their usual way, to discuss the events they had seen, to sleep over them, and hope for a return of a similar excitement.

Do they not bestow one human thought on that wretched victim of their mirth, who was made to run the gauntlet of fire?

Is there no touch of human sympathy for him?

Not a touch! Not a touch!

The eras of Augustus and of his successors, grand as they may be, are eras of the savage man, of tragedy in earnest, of martyrdom in sport, and of life altogether, as the dying Augustus himself defined it, life in comedy, in which the comedy of pain plays the choicest part.

To this civilisation the fate of Simeon the living torch is so small a subject of sympathy that the majority of the masses are inclined to complain because the whim of the Emperor permitted the youth to escape into the open country. Had Severus retained command, the torch might have been run in the large arena, round and round, until it had blazed out. Then, half-cooked for ravening wolves or bears, it might have been left in a fenced ring to fight with the animals one by one, until, unable to fight more, it yielded up its body to their devouring jaws.

Whether, as it is, he, the running torch, is suffocated in the smoke which rose from his body, or is roasted alive, or is lying like a hunted deer in ditch, or field, cr fence, to die by inches, is, to the masses, not worthy of a passing thought.

In a select few, however, his fate excites a different, if not a better feeling.

In Hadrian it excites a mystery which he trusts to time to explain.

In Severus it excites doubt, which he likes not, and which he is anxious to solve. At his command that troop of horse which called the companions of Tinnius Rufus out of the tent has gone forth to find the torch or his remains.

In Huldah does it excite no cause of concern, no anxiety?

Strangest even of all ! None !

Her soul communes with higher powers than men. She is a woman of faith that will remove mountains. She not only believes, but she knows that he whom she bade go on in the name she sang, and with the promises she delivered in that holy name, is under such shelter that he will take no harm. Literally, to her faithful eye, Simeon would go through the fire and not be burned, through the waters and not be overwhelmed.

Could he who was fore-known, fore-ordained ere ever the seas or the earth were made, or the light was separated from the darkness ; could he be left to perish? The very doubt were a sin, infamous and unpardonable,

against the God of her race, whose promises
are the same yesterday, to-day, and for ever.

She, moreover, has two other cares, which
occupy her thoughts.

Milo, the owner of the Numidian out of
whom she had cast the evil one ; Milo, disgusted
with the infirmity of his man-brute, has determined to sell the creature, at an immense loss,
to some young Romans who intend next day
to have him baited again for the Emperor's
private sport and theirs. If sold to them, he
is to fight more wolves with that massive
club, and wagers run high on the event.

The spirit that guides Huldah tells her,
without being asked, that the Numidian must
be saved.

She requires no further prompting. Sometimes, when she seeks the aid of the spirit
from her own earthly wishes, she doubts the
nature of the response ; it is ambiguous, it
leaves too much to her judgment, and is not
of faith. Then her heart is weak, and her
mind is borne down. But when the spirit
speaks of itself, when it says, without being
consulted, do this thing straightway, there is
no doubt, no delay. To save this man is there-

fore her first care and duty; but she has yet another care almost as pressing and severe.

On her return to the tent of Fidelis, after leaving the Circus Britannicus, she finds Fidelis, completely prostrated by the events of the day, lying on his couch, talking of men and things of whom she has no knowledge, as if she understood him.

The experience is new to her: she has never seen Fidelis tired or lying down except at his usual hour for rest; she has never heard him talk in that garrulous way; she has never before known him refuse to listen to her words of affection and trust, as he does now.

She has a duty to fulfil to this father of fathers, and she has a duty to fulfil to the man whom she has released from the power of the devil. To these duties she lends herself with a devotion which none but a nature such as hers could put forth.

In the midst of all Simeon remains on her mind, yet neither with anxiety nor fear. He is her true soul's care, but the Holy One is with him.

'Why,' she asks herself, 'why, whenever I

think of him, should the spirit, my spirit, say
these promises to me but to assure me?'

And so she is led to trust and perfect
peace.

Oh! happy they who, relying on such sure
foundation, found their every hope on the
God of their salvation.

Perchance, too, these favoured ones have
their soul's peace resting on natural law.
Perchance, in time, wise men will discover in
vital physics, and in the destinies accomplished
by them, that by natural ordinance, respecting
which there shall be no mystery, some of the
earth are ordained thus to live in immediate
communication with the eternal energy which
fills all life and speaks to the human heart
through the human soul.

To us, at all events, let Huldah remain
divinely assured that her beloved is, as she
believes, protected by the promise and the
power that none can overcome.

Let us also, leaving her for the time to her
beneficent tasks, resting on her promises and
cherishing them, follow him upon whom her
heart is fixed, and see how far her faith is fulfilled.

To effect this change in our programme it is necessary for us to go back to the time when Simeon, as the running torch, was led out to meet his great and fearful ordeal.

Our minds thus diverted naturally return to the strange and noble-looking man, who, with his angelic child, sat in the circus and wondered at the pleasure testified at so much sin and pain. With infinite anguish, which but for gentle outlets of tears had broken their hearts, the two had sat out the battle between Simeon, the Numidian, and the wolves. They had watched with untold wonder and relief the episode of the power of the dark and beautiful Huldah, rising from the feet of the Emperor, upon whom they looked with little favour, to accompany Simeon the condemned with cymbal and inspiring song. Towards her they turned their eyes with pious admiration, esteeming her as a being not only beautiful, but endowed with supernatural gifts and qualities.

But when they fully understood the fate that was in store for the youth, so handsome and so brave, their hearts gave way altogether. They had not conceived it possible that an act so foul could be committed ; and, powerless to arrest the iniquity, they did the best they could to show their utter detestation of it. They bound up their sandals, gathered their robes around them, and left the accursed place for ever.

When they had reached the outside of the grand circus, and saw once more the distant hills before them, the sobbing child found relief in words.

'Will they, dearest father,' asks the sweet voice, 'will they truly set on fire him who has done no wrong and been so generous? Will they indeed make his poor body a torch of living fire for their wicked sport and pleasure?'

'Alas! my child, I fear they will do, even with delight, whatever that monster human god who rules over them may choose to command.'

'And can we, dearest, do nothing to save him?'

'I have been forecasting that hope, my own, and foresee an opportunity. If he can leap the pit and run with sufficient speed across the valley leading from the eastern gate of the circus; if he can climb yonder hill; if he can reach on the other side that pool on the bank of which we said our morning prayers to the fountain of light and love ; and, if into that pool he can plunge, his danger might be over. Thither we will hasten to guide and help him.'

' But what if from weakness he should sink before he reaches the pool ? '

'We may even then see some plan by which to aid him. But let us away.' And, with the swiftness of spirits, they seem to fly, until they arrive at the little lake over the rising ground on which their minds have centred.

In the rushes that surround the pool some native had moored his light boat, made of slender rods of hazel or willow covered with skins of oxen, and holding within it the paddles, just as they in the morning had seen it.

' May I touch the boat ? ' sighed the child ; ' 'tis covered with the skin of a slain animal, and the paddles are stained with blood ? '

' Our sacred commandments teach that to save any human life all rules ordinarily held holy may be broken, since the human life is the purest part of the eternal fire from which we have our being.'

Withdrawing her gently from the margin of the pool, and instructing her what to do, the wise man, a leader of his race, draws out the canoe, places it in a position ready for it to be entered in a moment of time, and then returning to his child, moves with her to a point of vantage where they can look over the valley towards the encampment.

There they recline and watch with vigilant eyes.

Quickly the child's keen sight catches what they are looking for.

' See !' she cries, ' he is in sight ! he ascends towards us ! He approaches us like a blazing meteor traversing the earth. Let us kneel and pray.'

And, for a moment, they did kneel to their deity, imploring him fervently not to devour the innocent youth who bore his raging flame.

' He comes ! he lives ! he will be with us in an instant. Let us, dear father, lead him to the lake.'

' Go forward, my sweet one ; but not too near him, lest thy frail garments touch the

fire he carries. In the Roman tongue call to
him to follow thee as if thou wert a spirit in
his path ; so calling, flee thee to the canoe and
join me. He will follow us and live.'

Like a truly angelic being the child flies
towards the flaming Simeon, and, waving a
light scarf to fix his attention, calls out with
sweetest voice, ' Come, come ! Follow me!
Follow me ! '

In the strange confusion and excitement
of the moment, the living torch, though he
were of merest ordinary mould of mind, might
be excused if he believed that some more
than ordinary power had interposed on his
behalf. To him who felt himself fore-ordained,
the manifestation, if not an expected event at
that precise moment, is a perfectly reasonable
and probable occurrence sent and meant to
save him. To his firm set enthusiasm this
voice is but another of the voices of the night
on which his soul had from its first watches
fed, and, without hesitation, he follows the
spirit before him whithersoever it may lead
him.

Rapidly, still hearing the sweet call, ' come
come ! ' he sees the angel join another being of

resplendent beauty, sitting as it seems to him, the entranced, on a lake of crimson, over which both glide away beckoning him still to follow.

A hissing sound, like that the smith produces as he dips his heated metal in the trough, a cloud of vapour from the surface of the pool, and the living torch might have been transformed into a drowned man, but for the two strong arms and the assistance they afford. Soon he feels a powerful hand on his body helping him to rise from the water; a few moments more and he stands erect.

He stands a blackened mass, but safe and sound, breast high in the water, throwing his long black locks from off his face and gazing wildly at his deliverers.

'The prophecy is, indeed, fulfilled. "When thou walkest through the fire it shall not consume thee, through the waters they shall not overflow thee!"'

Above his head the stars are shining in radiant clearness; facing him one lustrous orb seems to fill him with her own glory; he hears the voices of angels who lead him through the river of life Zion-ward. Surely he will soon behold the city whose streets are paved with gold and where there is no death.

The expectation is false, as many other such have been before. When his feet rest on the shore, he hears the voices telling him, still in the Latin tongue, not to fear ; and soon they, in turn, are entranced as he raises his hands to heaven, and, in a language they seem to comprehend, pours forth his thanks.

> ' My heart is fixed, my heart is fixed.
> I will sing and give praise.
> I will praise thee, O Lord, among the people,
> I will sing unto thee among the nations.
> For thy mercy is great unto the heavens,
> And thy truth unto the clouds.
> Be thou exalted, O God, above the heavens.
> Let thy glory be above all the earth.'

They are sublime words, declarations uttered with the fervour of one inspired. They clothe a secret declaration that henceforth, through a life however short, however long, the message shall be uplifted as a banner to be read by all peoples :—

> ' Be thou exalted, O God, above the heavens.
> Let thy glory be above all the earth ! '

The listeners are as enraptured as the worshipper ; but one of them, ever wise and

prudent, reasons with himself that some enquiring followers from the camp will surely
pursue, and that ere the moon shall rise it
were well to study the best measures for complete escape from a place which to him is as
the confines of a world of sin and death.

'He sings, my father, he sings!' exclaims
the rapturous child; 'he must be well.'

'True, my own, all who can sing can live;
and observe that he offers his thanks to the
Omnipotent Power that has so far saved
him before he turns to the instruments that
omnipotence has employed. 'Tis according to
our own sacred law and the wisdom of our
blessed ancestors. It is as it should be.'

The declaration finished, Simeon for the
first time addresses himself to his deliverers,
to whom as beings of more than human
quality he bends in admiration.

The idea of their supernatural character
is dispelled by the extremely practical manner
in which the chieftain speaks to him.

'Thou hast done well, my son, to return
thy thanks to thy Omnipotent Lord. To
us, mortals like thyself, let no thanks be
given, save those which come from a true

and grateful heart, in deeds of truth and honour.'

With ready skill he once more places the little canoe in the rushes by the shore, as he had found it, obliterates all trace of footsteps and other signs of what has occurred during its use, and enquires with tender care, if he who has escaped so terrible a peril is fitted for further flight. To his satisfaction he finds that this is quite possible. From the rapidity of the flight of Simeon the bituminous covering on the sackcloth garment has alone blazed into fire, and the brisk wind which he has faced, blowing the flames behind him, has saved his face. The pouches or bags into which his hands and arms were thrust, are charred, so that he can force his hands through them, but his hands are not burned.

In a word, the intended victim, by simple natural causes alone, has escaped scatheless.

Seeing this with much delight, his wise deliverer calls his child, who, like a sentinel, watches the Roman camp, and, giving to her his right and to Simeon his left hand, he leads them into the night.

CHAPTER X.

IN THE CAP OF LIBERTY.

WHILST Simeon is being led away into the dark unknown, the Numidian, with whom his fate has been so singularly linked, is passing through another phase of his life, which, as having an important bearing on the future of this history, must occupy our exclusive attention in the present chapter.

Like an animal in a menagerie, the human animal from whom the demon has been cast out is lying in a kind of wooden stall or pen outside the camp, under a guard of camp-followers, who, as soldiers incapacitated by wounds from regular service, are now employed in watching the animals and men intended for the sports of the arena.

On the Numidian his guards look with a mixture of admiration and fear. They have disarmed him of his club; they have pacified him, as they think, by giving him an extra layer of clean straw for his bed. They have placed beside him a large leathern jug filled with pure water for his drink; and, from time to time, they have thrown to him scraps of food from their own table, in addition to the fare which Milo has provided for him.

Moreover, when they want him to get up in order to show his limbs or display his muscular feats to the gallants who come to inspect him, they command him in a gentler tone and gesture than is their custom, while they enter into his cell as rarely as is possible, and always with dainty vigilance.

For this Hercules incarnate, and lately possessed of a demon, is a captive whom it is considered wise to leave as much to himself as is convenient. He is a new experience altogether.

The next possible impending fate of the miserable wretch is known throughout the camp, and also to himself, for they who have come to look at him through the bars of his den talk as freely within his hearing about the ordeal he is likely to go through, as they do before the famishing animals which are to be his awful foes.

The proposition, as we have already seen, is that he shall next day fight again with wolves; and it is now suggested that he shall fight two sets of six each, one set after the other, in continued contest, for the enjoyment of the gallants who wish to purchase him, and who, of a wild and sporting character, are good representatives of certain of the oldest and most influential families of Rome.

The gallants drive a close bargain with Milo, and he, for he is notoriously a hard bargainer, with them. They survey the man they would purchase, at a respectful distance, from head to foot. They admit his herculean strength, but they dwell on that fatal flaw in his value, the demon that possesses him.

Milo, on his part, first maintains that the demon has been driven out of the animal.

'But will he guarantee that it will never enter him again,' they enquire. 'If he will there is his full claim with the penalty attaching to it should his guarantee fail.'

Not sufficiently certain of his case to accept these terms, Milo slily parries his offer as a joke, and in a half-hearted bantering tone, commonly assumed by all barterers in flesh and blood, praises the faults of the chattel he would sell.

'Mayhap the demon is at the bottom of all the skill which he possesses, and only throws him when he is doing wrong; therefore it were best it should come back to him.'

The gallants take this suggestion at its true worth, and thinking they have their man in a corner, they laugh, and leave him in order to join in the tumult incidental to the song of Tinnius Rufus, ' Ecce Imperator.'

The song over, they stroll about the camp as gallants will ; and when they feel that they have given Milo full time for reflection, they go to the tent of that crafty salesman to re-open the negotiation.

To their utter bewilderment, as they enter the tent, they discover the human animal who for their next morning's sport might be de-voured of wolves, clothed in Roman attire like their own, only of plainer stuff, and seated with Milo as at least his equal.

Divested now of all the barbarous trim-ming that have been put upon him for the

arena, he is a fine and stalwart man, of olive
complexion it is true, but of grand and noble
expression, and of graceful and even dignified
manner.

The gallants, there are four of them, cannot believe their senses. In their wonder they
rush back to the pen where the Numidian
had been confined.

The pen is occupied by six goats, which turn
towards them with mocking *baas*, shrill and
pressing, as if asking for the food they expect,
or the young of which they have just been
robbed.

For the fun of this night, and for the
matter of that of many other nights, the gallants have assumed to themselves the names
of Brutus, Cassius, Pompey, and young Octavius, characters supposed to suit and fit their
respective natures.

'By all the infernals,' lisps the young
Octavius, ' this change of animal out-Cæsars
Cæsar.'

' Another miracle!' exclaims Pompey.

' A beastly attempt to extort from us more
gold,' whispers Brutus.

' But not likely to succeed until we have

stripped the beast, and seen that we have not
been cajoled by a counterfeit,' urges the fiery
Cassius, as he draws his dagger-knife to rip up
the toga of the released Numidian, to whom,
while carrying on their exclamations, they
have furiously returned.

'Hold, gentlemen, hold!' interposes Milo.
'Who touches him touches Cæsar. He is
mine no longer. He has obtained his freedom,
ranks as a Roman citizen like ourselves, and
as his club is now his own weapon, it were
wiser for you to drink to his future success as
a freeman of Rome, than to quarrel either with
Cæsar or with him.'

And as Cæsar and the weapon of the newly
freed man are not things to be trifled with,
the gallants, like all men who are prudent as
well as gallant, throw themselves at once into
the humour of Milo, call for wine, and would
now drink to the new representative of freedom and power until break of day, did he not
check them.

'In the country from whence I come, noble
sirs,' he explains in a gentle but manly tone,
and with good Roman accent, 'in the country
whence I come my people use a bow which

no other people can bend. We live to one hundred and twenty years. In the days of our forefathers, King Cambyses and his son Cyrus feared to fight against us, and one of your own Cæsars failed to subdue us, though he took some of us captive. All our men are strong as I; our women, equally strong, are far more beautiful; and the secret of all our strength lies in one simple act. We take no stupefying food or drink.'

'By Bacchus!' whimpers the young Octavius, ' this is too blasphemous. I pray thee, Brutus! Cassius! Pompey! let us go to the temple! let us go to the temple!'

'And what,' asked Milo, when the exquisites had departed, 'what, thou fortunate of fortunate men, will be thy next promotion? I warrant thee thou wilt take for a wife this Jewish Huldah, and be more enslaved than ever. Women do not give freedom to handsome young athletes without trying to take them all to themselves.'

The suggestion, a mere random joke of a rough Roman soldier flushed with wine and newly primed with money, throws the freedman into a frenzy almost as demonstrative as

the seizure in the arena, an exhibition which
brings such fears to the affrignted Milo that
his red cheeks turn ghastly pale.

'Fear not,' responds his visitor encourag-
ingly, 'fear not, good Milo; the spirit which
so long haunted me is cast out for ever. But
thy saying struck deep into my heart and
transfixed it. Why, man, in all thy calendar
of Roman goddesses there is not one so divine
as she who gave me freedom. They call her
divine half in sport, half in fear. She is
divine! She is not mortal, nor is there mortal
man will ever dare to claim her as wife. Her
follower through life to death I may be; her
faithful companion, her tried servant, her
proven friend, but never more.'

And seeing the earnestness of the speaker,
and that there is no danger of a return of
the evil demon, the recovered Milo, who believes about as much in goddesses and divine
women as he does in a bad bargain, allows
the new freedman to relieve his full heart by
a copious flood of tears, without any interruption.

'Strange,' thinks Milo, as he busies himself
in putting things in order in the tent, and in

preparing a couch for the new occupant, 'strange that a Hercules like that should cry like a baby. I wage me that Severus, or those madcaps, or Tinnius Rufus—well, I'll not be too sure about Tinnius—or myself, would never cry like that at my words. Surely it was natural enough to suppose that a handsome young woman who gives all the money she possesses to buy a handsome young man, who was going to be turned into an ugly old wolf within twenty-four marks of the candle, would have him in her eye as something unusually excellent. Why not?'

Thus musing whilst he arranges the couches, and then sitting down on his own couch to unloose his sandals, Milo falls into a brief reverie on the events of the day now coming to a close, a day which has given a freedman to Rome, a worshipper to Huldah the Jewess, and a mint of money to his own exchequer.

Let us leave Milo absorbed in what is passing before his mental gaze, and go back a short time in order to disclose the mode in which the Numidian obtained his freedom.

We know already that Huldah had determined to save the man from whom, by some strange spell, she had cast the demon, and to whom, by some stranger spell still, she was attracted, as if by a mysterious hand which led her to resolve on his deliverance in a mode which shall, for a moment or two, occupy us as observers of a stratagem of fate.

Fidelis the Centurion of a hundred years has returned, as we have already seen, from the Circus Britannicus back to his own quarters a changed man. He is faithful as ever to all that a brave man holds most dear—his religion, his duty, his country, his friends.

These have ever been the four corner stones of his temple of life : RELIGION, DUTY, COUNTRY, FRIENDSHIP.

And on four sounder foundations has no man ever built.

The events of the day have, however, proved at last too much for his powers. The excitement of the triumphal march around the course ; the arrival of Hadrian, whom he had once escorted in the previous reign, and to whom, then an uncrowned man, he had ren-

dered useful service; the conduct of his protégé Simeon, the obstinacy of the youth, and
his fate; the miracle he had witnessed. These
have induced in him a foreboding sadness,
followed, for the first time in his life, by
prostration both of body and mind.

He listens to Huldah's conversation, after
a time, with a kind of vacant pleasure. and
when he notices her sadness, as she tells of the
use which he out of whom she had cast the
bad spirit was soon to be put, he becomes
variable in mood, now mirthful, then contem-
plative, in rapid succession.

No longer Fidelis, the centurion of Cæsarea,
unmoved and always ready, but a child of
children.

With resignation he lays down the vitis on
his couch, and the sturdy rod, as if conscious
of its own helplessness without him, falls to
the floor.

Oh, terrible omen! The vitis falls from
Fidelis to the earth.

Tell it not in the camp, for it is the end of
power.

After a while, raising himself, with Huldah
by his side, he takes her hand, and seem-

ing to recast his thoughts, led back by some recollections of his early career, he questions her.

'Child,' he asks, 'art thou still firm in the faith of thy fathers?'

Huldah bends her head, as if that act were alone sufficient to attest her firmness and sincerity, and with continued revival of memory he proceeds.

''Tis well, my child, 'tis well. Keep thy faith, keep thy faith. In body thou may'st bend to men, for they are of the kingdom of this world, but keep thy soul free and pure. Thy father died for his people. 'Twas my duty to lead him out to be crucified. Many times we had most friendly meetings, Roman soldier as I was, Jewish reader in the synagogue he. But he rebelled against Rome, and I had my duty to perform, which, sad towards him, did not prevent me saving thee and thy playmate under his charge, the youth Simeon. Henceforth you and Simeon were the children, the second children, of the childless Fidelis, for my own two children, boy and girl, together with the mother that bore them, one of thy people, were taken from me by accident, in the springtime of my manhood.

'Often, often did their mother read to me from the sacred book thou knowest so well, and though it was foreign to me it comforted me. Thy voice is like hers; tell me something from thy book.'

With cheerful obedience Huldah narrates to him in low and gentle chant the music of the early stanzas of the second Isaiah. She tells him of the Creator of the ends of the earth; who fainteth not, neither is weary; whose understanding is unsearchable; who gives power to the faint, and to them that have no might increaseth strength; before whom the youths faint and are weary, and the young men utterly fall. But they that wait upon Him renew their strength, mount up with wings as eagles, run and are not weary, walk and are not faint.

To the old man the sweet words and promises seem to give new vitality.

'He is a great King, Huldah, my child. He is a great King. I wish I were one of His centurions. I should like to travel to where

He is, and see Him in His noble palace, and show him the chaplet Severus put on my head when they called so loud my name. Let us go to Him. Let us go!'

The words fall from his lips like those of a little child about to take a journey to some spotless home, of which it has been told and which he dies to see.

Suddenly the mood changes, and matters of immediate importance cross his mind relating to the earthly future yet in store for her whose hand he holds.

'What, my child, can I do for thee?—what give thee besides the blessing of a man who has filled his years?'

'A life,' she replies, ' a life, dearest friend and protector! Give me a life that, once given, shall, I promise thee, be devoted, body, soul, and spirit, to that Lord and Master you would serve so faithfully.'

'Life! life! life! Is not that, maiden, in the hands alone of the great King?'

'Nay, 'tis in thine now,' she cries, as she looks imploringly into the bewildered face of the child of children. 'Thou hast influence, thou hast means. No one to-day will deny

Fidelis anything that thou hast means and will to ransom.'

And then, slowly and gently, that he might receive it all, she tells him the impending peril of the slave from whom she has cast out the unclean spirit, and claims his purchase for the service of the King of kings, whose worshipper she is.

It is a prayer easily granted—granted, in fact, with a smile and laugh of delight, as if it were a good piece of pastime or sport. Milo is sent for; his terms, not by any means extortionate to Fidelis, are accepted without demur; the bond is paid, and the man, once possessed of a demon, is bought and made over to the good angel who has been sent to accomplish his second deliverance.

She must lose no time in claiming what belongs now to her.

Exhausted with the efforts he has made, Fidelis sleeps like an infant, and Huldah issues forth from his tent on her mission of mercy.

The slave also sleeps. The last heartless bargainer for him has subjected him to the last inspection, and he has been shut up for the night, with the massive club dropped into two slots to form a bolt for the outer door of his den, and to act as a sign that this is the place in which he lies waiting for his fate.

After the bolt has thus been put up he, chained and securely fastened, disposes himself for rest. He rolls himself up into a ball and, as far as possible, buries himself in the litter of straw so that the noise of those howling wolves may be subdued. Unable to fall into slumber, yet feeling the need of it, he goes through the mental process of once more boldly meeting his foes in prospect, and of devising how he shall act so as to be saved. Shall he weary them each by flight, and kill them one by one as they lie at his mercy? They are too numerous this time for that. Shall he march up to each and with one crushing blow kill, kill, kill? 'Tis a bold idea, but too fatiguing and watchful even for him. He conceives next a method of meeting them by making a new series of springs or leaps, and so getting at them one by one, leaving the trusty club to do the rest. By this exploit, six of his enemies lie, in imagination, at his feet, and the new ones being let in, so ravenous they would devour the dead bodies of their kind were they not driven off with torches of fire, also fall. Then over a low part of the wall of the circus where the fight is going on he leaps with his club, and flies away after Simeon, the living torch, so swiftly that no one can catch him, and he is free in a strange land.

No, not quite strange either, for in the meadows over which he strides he reaches, he fancies, a land like that of his fathers. He meets an invading force, is captured, is held as a hostage ; is brought to some strange city and sold there as a slave ; is trained as an athlete ; is made to fight with real animals, wild and savage, and with men dressed up as animals ; is brought by his present master, Milo, to Britain ; is made to fight a Jew ; is cast, as he has often been, into a trance ; sees all the heaven open to his sight ; sees one of the host there come to him and relieve him ; is cast again into a den, and is doomed to-morrow to be devoured of wolves, whose voices ring in his ears.

The torture destroys itself. One can but die. And what is death ? Sleep is death, and deep sleep comes with the thought as if by inspiration.

As sleep vanquishes him his powerful muscles relax ; his limbs stretch out ; his head rests gracefully on his right arm ; his left arm, naked and strong, rests gracefully on his body ; around his body there still remains a portion of the skin of the bear in which he fought by the side of Simeon ; while round his neck is a white flowing under-vest, the collar of which, turned back as it was wont to be when he stood in the slave market, discloses a throat chiselled to perfection, above a chest of tremendous power, moved by gentle breathings deep, steady, and regular as the march of a cohort.

His face, compared with what it was in the arena, is now transfigured. The dark colour with which it had been treated in order to give it dense blackness has been removed : the red colour with which the lips and eyebrows were tinted has also been removed, and now there is revealed that face of singular power and grace which, by anticipation, we have already beheld as a face at peace with its own heart and with all the world.

Wrapt in a dark toga, to shield her from common observation, Huldah approaches with

Milo to the den of the sleeper. As they enter the gates of the menagerie, she, strong of will as she is, is appalled; for the noise of the ravenous animals rises to a frenzy, as Milo strikes his flint and lights his lamp. In a moment, all sense of fear is absorbed in the intent she has in view. In haste to fulfil her mission and release her slave from his bondage, she seizes the lamp which Milo holds out to her, and, impatiently waiting while he lights another for himself, follows him to the den bolted by the club.

Taking in hand both lamps, as Milo removes the heavy bolt and delivers it over to the sturdy keepers who are on watch outside, and holding the lamps raised and forward from her body, she enters the cage.

'There he is,' observes his late master, as she brings the lamps to shine on him, 'there he is, as fine a slave as ever was born. If he should go on sleeping like that until sunrise, he could beat every wolf and bear in the encampment, bringing back all the money he has cost, and sleeping to-morrow night again like a babe in his cradle, just as he is sleeping now.'

Huldah, too absorbed in what she sees
to listen to the suggestion, recalls, with the
admiring wonder of a woman for every living
source of strength her Eastern poetry.

'I am black but comely, O ye daughters of Jerusalem ;
  As the tents of Kedar, as the curtains of Solomon.'

'I must,' she communes, 'wake him from
this deep oblivion ; but how graceful his
rest !' Then, questioning if he really can be
the beast who fought with Simeon, she turns
to Milo and enquires :

'Is this indeed the man from whom I cast
the unclean spirit ?'

'The same. See you how the skin of
the bear still clings to his body ; but his arms
being uncovered and the dyes being off his
face, he becomes quite a different man.'

She is satisfied with the answer, but still
lingers ere she inquires further :

'By what name is he rightly called ?'

'He has been called by various names, according to the feats he has done or according
to the whim of his masters ; but the name he
originally bore, as I have been told, was Helios,
meaning that he came from the land of the
east, and where it is said his father, who was

the leader of the people there, was slain in a
great battle with Trajan, who was beaten, but
who, by accident, fell, during his retreat, on
the chieftain's children and carried them away
captive.'

The name and the story struck her, for a
moment, mute, as if she had heard that name
before and that history. Then, as she pon-
dered she recalled to her ready memory that
in the Scriptures she had learned the name
of Elias. But Elias was Elohim who made
the world, and this was Helios, after the
fountain of light which fills the world with
his glory and vivifies it with his power.
This man may be truly descended from her
race.

She kneels gracefully by his side, and
giving one of the lamps to Milo, who there-
upon wanders away to appease his ravening
wolves by throwing to them just sufficient food
to prevent them devouring each other, she is
left alone with the child of the East, her dark
mantle folded about the lower half of her
body, her white toga trimmed with gold en-
robing her shoulders and breast, her raven hair
falling over her back, and her dark eyes flash-

ing their rays over his face as the lamp she holds aloft feeds them with its light.

And now another of the mysterious passages with which she is so richly stored crosses her mind :

' Oh that thou wert as my brother that sucked the breasts
    of my mother !
When I should find thee without I should kiss thee :
Yea, I should not be despised.'

By an impulse irresistible as it is natural, as if the words inspired the act, she bends over the sleeper, and with the softest kiss that woman's lips can give, and with a touch and voice which might almost have aroused the dead, arouses him from his slumber.

It is a cruel awakening. He has fallen back to a past preceding his captivity, when in his blissful home he has gone forth with the morning sun to see the attendants milk the goats. He has with him his younger sister and still younger brother; they have sipped the sweet milk from the gourds, they have rolled with the young kids on the green sward, and one of the kids, which is very fond of him, is pushing its nose between his arm and side to ensure recognition, when he hears his mother, to him a divinity of love and beauty, calling to him sweetly in the distance :—

'Eli, Eli, come !'

It is the name which she, in a mother's loving tattle, has contracted for him from the longer and harder Helios.

'Eli, Eli, come !'

Is he again possessed?

Is it a return of the old, old trance, he asks of himself as he wakes from the enchantment.

No, it is her kiss on his baby cheek ; it is her voice once more.

Eli, Eli, come !'

'Ah, my mother ! my mother ! my mother ! Leave me not again for ever,' he sobs forth as his heavy eyes open overflowing with tears ; and that mother's voice in its own almost forgotten language repeats :

'Eli ! Eli ! come !'

Again the close foul den is manifest to his awakening senses. But how changed the scene ! The howlings of the wolves have ceased ; the darkness has fled ; and there is one over him celestial with celestial light, who speaks his native tongue, who knows his child's name in its childish form, whose face, whose voice, whose smile, is all of all to him again.

He is seized with an overwhelming desire. The desire forthwith to die.

But before that desire has taken form he is raised to full activity of life by the action of Huldah and the entrance of Milo.

Milo unlocks his fetters, Huldah gently helps him to rise, and casting some folds of her dark mantle over her shoulders, presents him 'per epistolam,'—by letter,—with the deed which tells him he is henceforth a freedman by the act of Fidelis the centurion.

Bearing the epistle of freedom clasped to his breast, and, marvel of marvels, led forth by the hand of its celestial messenger, he is soon in the presence of the centurion of a hundred years, who with the true delight of a child calls him Libertinus—the Freedman—and invests him with the badges of his freedom : the cap of liberty, the white robe, and the ring.

Libertinus! A Freedman! A Roman under the protection of Cæsar. A man, no more to be bought, no more to be sold.

Libertinus! A Freedman! no more to fight

as a beast with men, nor as a man with beasts
unless by a will which, for the first time since
he knew it and its worth, is his own!

Libertinus! A slave, whose soul belonged
to others and baser souls, set free; a soul of
man set at liberty! What inexpressible reality!
A man always free could never understand
the transformation.

Libertinus! A Freedman. The lowest
slave, lowest born by descent, a slave of
slaves, is bewildered by the boon! What,
then, a man of noblest nature and most
steadfast mind whom no lowness infects, no
cruelty stains, no danger appals!

We, who know nothing but freedom, can
never know his joy. He is born again. Born
to a new world, new hopes, new fears, new
loves, new life.

Milo invites the Libertinus, the Freedman,
to his own tent, to take up his abode there for
awhile, for which privilege Milo, we may be
sure, is well paid. Milo is always well paid.

No wonder that Milo, who values all things
and all men, and all women and all children,
by their money's worth, should venture to sug-

gest to his visitor, now re-named Eli Fidelis, that a woman's love had bought him a freedom which he must sell again to the woman.

No wonder that Milo, as he sits on his couch unlacing his sandals after the gallants have left his quarters, looks furtively at Liber tinus, and is for once in his life at his wits' end to discover what it can all mean, if neither love nor money be at the root of a transaction that crowns his once monster slave in the cap of liberty.

CHAPTER XI.

MOVING on in the course of our story, we must for a time quit the little island of Britain, and proceed to another and very different place. To all the friends or acquaintances we have made on the island we will for a short time say farewell. Fabius and Vibullius have gone for an excursion to the northern parts of the island, to visit the barbarians there, and take notes for a book of travel, which the learned Fabius means to write if his industry should ever equal his leisure. The renowned Saserna remains at his post, busier than ever. The gallants, the young Octavius, Brutus, Cassius and Pompey, rest a little from our further cognizance, with hopes that as they grow older they may amend. The pious Aaron of the Altar, and his neighbour the good old Priest of the Temple of Apollo,

continue with their people in discharge of
their duties, both, for a time, dead to our
new life. Milo the bartering soldier, who
knows how to turn over honest coin so
cleverly, and grumbles to himself that Cæsar,
who has no taste for sport, is no good for his
business, must also pass out of mind.

The whole island of Britain soon fades
from us as we set forth on our journey.   It is
a wild coast; it is a beautiful little land with
white cliffs planted in the sea; it is a mere
speck in the sea; it is as lost to our sight as
if it were submerged in the waters which we
traverse on the wings of our imagination.

We have left behind us, far away, an island,
and approach now the shores of the great
ocean in the middle of the world.   We land
in a new place.   The spirit that guides us tells
us that it has brought us to Joppa, the seaport
of Jerusalem.

This Joppa, or Jaffa, is an ancient town, and
is occupied by a very curious admixture of
peoples.   It was built by Solomon the Wise
before he erected, under the skill of Hiram
Abiff the grand architect, the holy Temple
of the Holy City.   It was the fate of Hiram

Abiff to die by the hands of three of his men, designated craft masons, because he would not communicate to them, on their rude and insolent demand, some of the higher mysteries of his calling; and these men, after they had killed him and buried his body in the earth, fled towards Joppa and concealed themselves in a cave near by, where they were found by the Menatschin or Prefects, whom the King had sent out to trace them to their hiding-place. The cavern remains to this day, and is one of the antiquities of the city, as we soon discover.

At Joppa, as the seaport of Jerusalem and of the land of ancient and sacred mystery to the Jewish nation, all the great importations from abroad are landed. It is a town of merchants, strangers, and scholars, and for many ages has held this distinctive history. Conquered by the Romans, after the destruction of the city and Temple of Jerusalem by Vespasian, it has become an important Roman station, and gradually under the united influences of Roman occupation, Phœnician commerce, foreign communication, and Jewish tenacity of purpose, is now a second Alexandria, in which an immense number of schools, chiefly

Jewish, flourish and yield as many scholars as the Roman Governor, Servien, can well keep under control with all his legions.

There is at this time amongst many other synagogues of the Jews in Joppa one renowned wherever the Jewish people travel, renowned to them and to theirs. The crowds are now filling it. Crowds of Romans, Greeks, and Persians are entering it. Jews of every kind, from the students of the schools to the men and elders, and women of all ages, are making for it eagerly.

Lucilla, the wife of Servien the Roman Governor, prays her husband that she may go, and Servien assents, with the wish that it were compatible with his place that he might accompany her.

For the message has gone forth that Akiba, the chief of the Jewish Grand Sanhedrin is to preach to the people.

'In his voice there is music; in his words there is wisdom; in his soul there is poetry; in his heart there is truth.'

So doth Lucilla, the wife of Servien the Governor, report to her lord as she starts for the synagogue.

No wonder that such a multitude crowds to hear the word which Akiba preaches. Music, wisdom, poetry, and truth, are the master powers of man universal: blended in one man they declare a man of men.

There is a Jewish school in Joppa for the Jewish youth. After the schools of Alexandria, on the plan of the best of which it is founded, this is the most famous school of the world.

Why?

Akiba, the chief of the Grand Sanhedrin is the chief of it. That is enough.

In this school Akiba takes his supreme delight. He loves the synagogue, he enjoys the reading of the sacred word: the Isaiahs are to him as waters of life which nourish the soul; Micah is as a fire which purifies; and Solomon is as an art which glorifies the living temple of the Most High.

But the school is still his choicest treasure. There he is the potter moulding the vital clay of twelve thousand scholars into whatsoever vessels of honour he chooses them to be. In the school he constructs the future of his race.

All men call Akiba the Rabbi, or simply

Akiba. There are many others called Rabbi, but he is the Rabbi of his people. To call him a chief Rabbi would reduce his power to commonplace.

On him fifty years sit easily. Akiba will live a hundred and thirty years like our father Israel, is the commonly accepted prediction amongst the Jewish community; a prediction so often made that it becomes an ordinary saying, accredited and passed from mouth to mouth, and concentrated into such entire belief, that they who assume that their own lives will needs be of shorter span beg, as their special request, that Akiba will admonish and guide their progeny even to the unborn generations.

There is much in Akiba of a personal kind which supports these ideas of superhuman excellency.

He shows no trace of age. His step is elastic, his figure erect, his laugh, his play, his prayer as vigorous as that of a youth of prime maturity. Amongst the pupils of the great school he is a pupil rather than a master, yet reverenced as he is loved.

All Israel that is near to him sends its sons

to be taught of him ; and as wealth is the last
of his desires, distance alone severs him from
the whole of his people who would be his
children.

To him also come the learned men, the
masters of the law, and the prophets, that they
may help him in composing and editing a
marvellous commentary that is to go forth as
a new and second testament and interpretation,
by proverb, discourse and legend, of the old
Scriptures that were written by inspiration.
These doctors and ' disciples of the will,' men
of humble life and occupation, come to him
by night with their untold stores of learning,
to read under his guidance and be guided by
his matchless light.

But the greatest power of all that is connected with this man, and that establishes his
influence, is a story, already transformed into
a pious legend, in which he is represented.

Who wrote this legend is unknown. Some
say it was a beloved pupil whose severe studies
cost him his life. Others declare that a wise
woman found the story in the ruins of the
Temple in the holy city of Jerusalem. A
third set affirm that it came from the pen of a

mysterious man banished in a lonely island,
who gave it forth, in prophetic strain, and was
heard of no more.   From whomsoever derived,
it is to the oriental mind of Shemite birth as
bewitching a story as ever was told of any
man of woman born ; a story next only in
wonder to that of Enoch, Elijah, Abraham,
Moses, Samuel, and the others who had com-
muned with the angel.

And he whose mysterious knowledge is
told in this record still lives amongst the living;
preaches in the synagogue ; teaches in the
schools ; presides over the Grand Sanhedrin
or council of Israel ; and, meeting his people
daily in the streets and houses, is one with
them.

A man of human form like other men, but
of superhuman experience ; a man whose feet
have trodden ground which none since the
first days of man on this earth have trodden;
whose eyes have rested on wonders which no
man since the first man has seen ; whose ears
have heard a celestial voice and answered it ;
and who yet lives, and moves, and breathes
amongst his fellow-men.

The very heathen are influenced. Servien,

the Roman Governor, is walking one day to the baths in company with the princely Fortunatus, the bosom friend of the Emperor. They pass Akiba, and Fortunatus, a visitor to the Governor and fresh to Joppa, is, like the rest of the world, struck with admiration, as if touched by some secret power, when Akiba goes by.

'Who,' asks the ever-inquisitive stranger. 'who is this mysterious man?'

'He,' replies the Governor—'he is the most learned of all the Jews, the chief of their priests.' And dropping his voice, adds: 'they say of him that he is the only man who has entered their Paradise or the garden of innocence and come out of it alive.'

'Is he one of the sect,' enquires Fortunatus, 'of those some call Christians?'

'Of none akin, neither by relationship. name nor creed.'

'I am glad of it. In Bithynia those people called Christians gave our once great friend, the second Pliny, when he was proconsul there, so much trouble, he had to write to Trajan concerning them. They literally

emptied the temples of our gods by their
heretical worship.'

'This man is none of them. He follows
the ancient faith of his fathers, expounds their
sacred Scriptures, and is from head to foot an
ancient Jew according to what they call the
law of Moses.'

'I know that name as of the Jew who
wrote a history of the creation of the world,
and whom the Alexandrian Philon Judæus hath
commented on. But this man and follower
of Moses the great, what is his name?'

'Akiba.'

'How dost thou spell it?'

And Fortunatus, taking from his breast
his tablet and stylus commits the name, as
Servien spells it out, to what he calls his
' second memory.'

'And this legend about him and the garden,
what of that?' he asks, still holding the tablets and stylus as if he would also write that
down.

'Thou shalt hear for thyself, thou greedy
scholar; for know thou that my wife is so
affected to these Jews, having their blood in
her veins, that she will often herself have this

legend told before her as a sacred drama,
in which four voices speak the parts. Thou
shalt hear it this very night. Marah, Eri,
Tirzah, and Jachin, the first and third women,
the second and fourth men of our court, shall
speak the parts in character.'

CHAPTER XII.

A LEGEND OF PARADISE.

In the reception hall of the Roman Governor of Joppa, Servien, sometimes called Facilis, because of the gentleness of his nature.

In the presence of Servien and of Lucilla, his beautiful wife ; in the presence of Fortunatus, the bosom friend of Hadrian the emperor ; in the presence of the chief officers of the household of Servien, and of the army of occupation.

When the dinner has been completed and the wine has ceased to be tasted.

When the sun has gone down and the great hall of reception is lighted with many lamps, perfumed with waters of sweetest odour, decorated with choicest flowers and cooled with the gentle breezes from off the surface of the sea of mid earth.

When the slaves have placed themselves

at the doors and curtains so that none may intrude to disturb the story.

When Lucilla has taken the seat of honour between Servien and Fortunatus, and when all the guests and household are seated.

When the players on the lutes have finished their strain.

When the master of the ceremonies has motioned all to silence, and has given the sign that the story may begin.

Then, clad in rich and picturesque Eastern garments :—

Marah, Eri, Tirzah, Jachin, enter into the presence through an alcove of flowers, and on the floor of marble apportioned to them deliver their story :—

'The Legend of Paradise.'

From the right hand, Marah, in pure and plaintive tones, delivers an invocation to some distant hidden power. Then, turning to the audience, she explains the intention of him who has invoked the unseen.

As her part ceases Eri, whose voice sounds as from afar, declaims, from a point in the centre farthest from the audience, the answer of the mysterious being, who is called the Cherubin, to the words of the invocation.

Next, from the left-hand side, the gentle Tirzah relates in four simple lines, and in a tone that almost reaches song, the progress of the events.

Finally, with an emotional energy and mystery which no one but an Eastern could sustain, Jachin declares the result in a voice that penetrates to the very marrow of the listeners, and fills the delighted Fortunatus with enthusiastic admiration.

The parts fit the characters as if by nature. Marah's grace is of prayer, solemn, intense, eager. Eri is keen, commanding, fearful. Tirzah is slow, timorous, doubtful. Jachin is strong, decisive, bold.

And now their task begins.

I.

MARAH.

Oh mighty Cherubin, with flaming sword
Before the gate ! Before, before the gate !
   Touchless with human hands,
   Sightless with human eyes,
Portal of sinful mortal fate,
   The gate of Paradise !
Oh mighty Cherubin, speak but the word !

That I may see the garden of the Lord
  And grow more wise.

Thus spake the First of four of men who were
The living pillars of the deathless race.
Ezra! the scholar and interpreter
Of the great book of life which time shall ne'er efface.

ERI.

Then from the flaming sword
Came forth the sacred word,
Enter thou faithful one;
Thy work hath been well done,
Enter the garden of the Lord.

TIRZAH.

Beyond the sword of fire,
Untouched by fire or sword,
He gains his soul's desire,
The garden of the Lord.

JACHIN.

That he may grow more wise
He enters Paradise.
Enters! Beholds! and Dies!

II.

MARAH.

Oh dreaded Cherubin, whose flaming sword
Doth hide from mortal eyes the stream of life!
The tree of good and evil and its fruit;
The place where God breathed into man his breath;
The place where God and man spake word to word;

Where every living plant and herb and brute,
Was given man ; and from him torn the wife
Whom the foul serpent led aside to death.
Oh dreaded Cherubin ! grant my desire
Unquenchable as thy consuming fire,
   Which guardeth Paradise !
That I may see the garden of the Lord
   And grow more wise.

Thus spake the Second one who reached the goal.
Asaph ; a mystic form who shone,
As if his eager soul
Incarnate, would be gone ;
Leaving its fleshly dress
In this world's wilderness.

ERI.

Straight from the lambent flame the words were said ;
   If that thou fearest not to see
What made a brother scholar like to thee
   Fall with the dead ;
Killed by the glory he could not survive.
   Then, true and faithful one !
   Whose work hath been well done !
Enter the garden of the Lord, and live.

TIRZAH.

Beyond the sword of fire,
Untouched by fire or sword,
He gains his soul's desire,
The garden of the Lord.

JACHIN.

That he may grow more wise
He enters Paradise.

Enters ! beholds from whence
They were expell'd who did at first transgress.
Enters, beholds and flies
Back to the wilderness,
Bereft of every sense !

III.

MARAH.

Lo ! glorious Cherubin with flaming sword !
Lo ! I Elisha Ben Abuyah stand—
Stored with all learning gained in every land—
Before the gate whence Eve and Adam fled ;
Asking of thee that I may freely tread
   The plains of Paradise.
That I may see the garden of the Lord
   And grow more wise.

Thus spake the Third in tones of majesty ;
Elisha Ben Abuyah, who would pierce
The solid earth, the sea, the eternal space.
Not suppliant but as a Deity,
Asking from God of God ! As face to face
A ravenous man, feeling his hunger fierce,
Asks man to feed him to satiety.

ERI.

Again the voice from out the flaming sword.
Thou son of subtlety and earthly pride !
Wherefore within thy mantle's flowing folds
Dost thou those books of Baal worship hide ?
Our God, a jealous God, for ever holds
Him lost to him who serveth him in part,
Giving the lip, yet keeping back the heart.

Elisha Ben Abuyah stood dismayed,
But gathering up his strength and bending low
Thus to the flaming Cherubin he said.
These treasured books, dear as my own heart's blood,
I burn! I burn! I burn! that I may know
The greater secret that before me lies,
The garden of the Lord saved from the flood,
    The golden Paradise.

The flaming fire rose up and filled the skies :
    A burning sacrifice
Of all Elisha Ben Abuyah loved.
It is enough, the Cherubin replies,
Thou art forgiven, is the gracious word.
And, every barrier to thy wish removed,
    Enter the garden of the Lord.

TIRZAH.

Beyond the sword of fire,
Untouched by fire or sword,
He gains his soul's desire,
The garden of the Lord.

JACHIN.

That he may grow more wise
He enters Paradise.
Boldly he looks around,
And treads the holy ground
As one who would declare,
I am the son and heir
Of him to whom these treasures all belong.
Rivers of life combine,
With the fruit of the Tree divine,
To nourish with marvels my tongue.

Of all that is here, as mine,
I will sing! I will write! I will tell!
From the gates of heaven to hell:
In parable, legend and song.

Filled with the curse of pride
Elisha Ben Abuyah makes his way,
Crushing with reckless stride
What'er before him lay.
Crushing the tender plants so young and sweet,
The plants of Paradise, beneath his feet.

What voice is that he hears,
That breaketh him with fears?
What pang is that he feels?
It is the voice of God,
The angel's flashing rod.
Oh thou who kills the plants of Paradise
That thou, vain man, may grow more wise!
Fly from my wrath back to the wilderness,
And seek again thine everlasting peace.

A lightning glance! a split of earth! a grave!
    Outside the flaming gate.
Elisha Ben Abuyah, who shall save
Thee from thy fate?
In flight he falls into that open grave,
And as the flint upon the steel
Strikes into fire, so he upon the ground
Bursts into lurid flames, which he can feel
Yet never can extinguish. Years roll round;
Ages of sons of men sink down and die.
    Elisha Ben Abuyah to be wise
Killed the young plants of Paradise.
His light is wisdom's fool. He burns but never dies.

IV.

MARAH.

Oh faithful Cherubin whose flaming sword
Doth hide the garden of the Holy One !
May I, a shepherd born in Israel's fold,
Ask thee to ask of him I dare not name,
Th' Omnipotent!   World without end the same !
That I the last of those who stood alone
Interpreters of his most sacred word,
May through thy glory enter Paradise,
And by thy radiant wisdom grow more wise ?

So spake the last of those who stood alone,
The matchless scholars of the deathless race.
Calm dignity from off his image shone,
Sweet modesty was written on his face,
With courage intermixed and gentle grace,
    All set in comeliness.

ERI.

With cheerful voice the guardian spirit spoke :
Akiba the beloved, thy deeds are known.
He whom thou servest through thy nights and days
Hath read thy heart of hearts and seen thy ways.
Thou art to him a plain and open book,
And what thou askest now is all thine own ;
Thine own for knowledge, wisdom, precept, word.
    Enter thou to the garden of the Lord.

TIRZAH.

Beyond the sword of fire,
Untouched by fire or sword,

He gains his soul's desire,
The garden of the Lord!

JACHIN.

That he may grow more wise
Akiba enters Paradise.
His feet retrace each round
Of the enchanted ground,
Saved only of all gardens from the flood.
The tree of knowledge yields him living food.
Within the bower where Adam slept he sleeps
Fearing no evil: knowing well that He,
 Of omnipresent majesty!
The Holy One of Israel! keeps
His steps from falling and his sleep from fear,
Life of his life: unseen yet ever near.

That he might grow more wise,
Akiba entered Paradise.
Entered and lived and learned.
And when his wondrous task was done
Back through the wilderness returned,
To teach to every chosen son
Of Israel born, the sacred mysteries.

The reciters retire: the guests depart
from the house of Lucilla and Servien, one
alone excepted, the princely Fortunatus. He,
for the moment, the resident guest of the
house, remains wrapped in fixed contempla-
tion of what he has just seen and heard.

CHAPTER XIII.

THE LEARNED CHILD.

SERVIEN, so soon as he can be spared, makes his escape to his duty. He goes forth to see with his own eyes that his sentinels are at their posts. Nothing escapes his watchful ken. His soldiers say he never sleeps. The Jews repeat the saying, and well they may, for he observes them, specially, by night as well as by day.

There is sufficient cause for his anxiety. The Jews are placed, by the chances of war, under the powerful hand of Rome; they are subdued, but they are not conquered.

A race is never conquered until it is exterminated. It comes up like a flower, it is cut down and withered; but it comes up again and flourishes unless its roots and seeds be destroyed.

And now in Joppa twelve thousand youths

of the subdued race, twice the number of the Roman soldiers there, are at the schools for Jews ; youths filled to their souls' full charge with the traditions of their fathers ; ready at a moment's notice to rise and do whatsoever Akiba should command. If they should rise up and use no other weapons than the styles with which they write, they were formidable. If they were armed with weapons of war, they were invincible.

Happily, weapons are not permitted to them.

Akiba, moreover, is a wise and prudent father. He has gathered around him other scholars like to himself who have made learning a field of combat, which turns, as Servien feels, a war of swords into a war of words. These scholars labour incessantly on the sacred Jewish Scriptures. They translate their Scriptures from their ancient tongue into Greek, and even into Latin. They do more, they ' search the Scriptures,' and out of them, with endless activity, they learn the meaning of words, to the minutest understanding of every word ; they extract from obscure parts traditional laws ; they turn the prophetic parts to their own modern use by the exposition of legend and parable; and they add to the whole the study of those secret and holy mysteries which appeared to ' him who saw the glorious vision of the Creator and of the Chariot' and who by his learning and poetic imagination was the prince of seers, the divine Ezekiel.

They labour to perfect and advance a book of the ages, which commencing in Babylon is to continue to the end of the world.

A truly harmless task, according to the ideas of Servien and his compeers.

Let them read, write, learn and teach, and all will go well.

One thing more has Akiba done which carries with it confidence. He has taught the different classes of his countrymen many useful arts. A traveller through various climes, he has studied metals, furnace work, and other strange devices of men. He has learned and taught the manufacture of spears, swords, arrow-heads and shields.

Under strictest supervision of the Roman power, he has saved his poorer students from revolt, due to destitution, by giving them work in the manufacture of arms for the

Roman legions ; arms so chaste, so bright, so light, so beautiful, the like of them has never been seen before. The javelins literally fly. Servien therefore keeps the students of Akiba in his regular employ making arms which, with the exception of a few prepared for the use of his own bodyguard and for one or two officers of high rank, as test weapons, are jealously stored away to be of use should an insurrection ever break out.

'They make lances for their own flesh, and I keep them,' is a constant delight in secret of Servien, who in his heart admires as much as he pities Akiba, ' the learned child,' whom much learning has driven mad. He congratulates himself, and Rome also, whenever he passes the well-sentinelled armoury where the precious weapons lie, that he has turned the skill of so learned a child to so good an account. He has reported this clever stroke of policy and stratagem to the Emperor, who has written back to him commending his foresight and ability. The Emperor has said to him in special terms of commendation : ' If thou canst make these Jews quarrel amongst themselves about words and books while they make swords for thee, thou hast outwitted even a Jew.' What higher compliment, brave Servien, could be paid to thy prudence and thy strategy?

Whilst this crafty commander of Rome, who bids fair to beat a Jew in subtlety, and who is as honest of soul as he is brave and simple of heart, makes his nightly walks, his adored wife, surrounded by her maids, remains with Fortunatus awaiting his return.

The conversation of Lucilla and Fortunatus turns almost necessarily, certainly naturally, on the remarkable man whose legendary adventure has just been told to them in so dramatic a form.

'Putting aside this curious legend, noble lady,' observes her visitor, 'in which we shall or shall not believe according to our faith or our philosophy, what is the real story of this singular being about whose life there must needs be something that is really and authentically important?'

'There are as many stories, Fortunatus, told about Akiba as there are moons in the year. But one of the many is dearest to me because it contains the tale of his lowly origin, his path to immortal fame, and above all his true and constant love.'

'In short, it is a love story, my noble lady, such as is most precious to a woman's heart.'

'I confess it to be true, but even to thee it might be pleasant, if, till Servien—who always likes to hear it—returns, thou wouldst listen to it thyself.'

'With avidity, most thoughtful of hostesses ; a love story is to me the essence of love, better perchance than the thing itself.'

'Fie ! Forunatus, fie ! thou wilt be caught in thy own net one day. Marah, my child, will it tire thee after all thy exertions to read, once more, the story ? '

'It will delight me, mistress of my heart, to do thy will ; and know thou, noble lord, that the story is written in my lady's own hand, though she tells it not herself.'

'I divined as much. What callest thou the story ? '

'We call it the Shepherd and the Princess.'

CHAPTER XIV.

THE SHEPHERD AND THE PRINCESS.

WHEN Sisera was commander of the army of Jabin, king of Tyre, he sent back to their native Galilee Joseph, of the family of Abraham, and Naomi, his wife.

And Jabin the king approved of the act of Sisera, but why he did remains unknown unto this day, for Jabin was a good king, whose ear was open to the complaints of all his people, whether native or mere sojourners, and this proceeding seemed unjust because no charge was brought either against the man or his wife that they had broken the laws of the kingdom.

What is still more strange, they were not sent forth penniless or empty-handed. They had provisions given to them for a long journey, and they had money given to them sufficient to purchase a flock for the desert.

But this was required of them, that they should avoid all places where men live in cities, and that they should pitch their abode in some remote and secluded place where they should rear flocks of their own, or tend the flocks of some others who had flocks that called for a shepherd.

The place required by the exiled Joseph and his wife Naomi was not long waited for. Amongst the merchant princes who traded between Tyre and Judea was one called Chuva, a Jew by birth, and still young, who had recently married a wife descended from the royal line of David, once a mighty king in Israel; and the wife of Chuva, having pity on the exiles, prayed of her lord that he would find them a dwelling-place.

Now Chuva loved his wife of royal blood more than his wealth, and her wish was his law. So he provided the exiles with a tract of his own lands in a far-off place in the plains of Carmel, and Joseph became the shepherd of Chuva the merchant of Tyre and Judea, who afterwards was one of the chief men of the holy city of Jerusalem.

The humble shepherd and his wife, so far

from lamenting their fate, were, as it seemed, glad to exchange the life they had hitherto led for their new home on the solitary plain. They, too, were young and but newly married, and they set out as for a marriage tour, dearly beloved of each other, and trusting in the God of their fathers, the God of Abraham, of Isaac, and of Jacob who was also called Israel.

In the wilderness, or plain in which they went, they lived as shepherd and shepherdess the long days of their natural life. Only at times, when all Jews go up to the Holy City to pay their vows to the Most High God, did they go from their place of duty; and not even then until their only son was old enough to tend the flocks while they were away.

For soon after Joseph the shepherd and Naomi the shepherdess had settled down in the plain, Naomi bore to Joseph a son, who at first took the name of his father the shepherd, Joseph; but his mother, under the spirit of heaven which directs the souls of the faithful, was led to call him by the Tyrian name of Akiba, which is said to mean the only one, or the only son, under which name she

prophesied that he was to be their only
child.

And the prophecy was fulfilled. Akiba
was the only child born to Joseph the shepherd
by Naomi his wife.

Thus the birth of Akiba was very humble,
and in some manner, as many think, mysterious
also; for why were his parents driven from
Tyre for no known offence, and at the same
time loaded with gifts and money?

The wisest man of men, Akiba himself,
does not know, how then shall a foolish
woman divine? She will be silent, and will
not try to interpret the unknown.

The lad Akiba was born in the desert,
in the plains of Carmel, and having to tend
the flocks kept by his parents, breathed the
breath of the Lord in the solitudes of his
loftiest temple, the temple in which his honour
dwelleth, the temple whose foundations are
set on the four corners of the earth, and whose
covering is the mantle of his glory. And in his
holy wisdom and pleasure this Lord of Lords
was gracious to the youth, and, as we say,
'called him,' so that he was from his cradle
beloved of God as well as of his parents and

of all whom he chanced to meet, during the many years he lived in the desert, an obedient son, and good shepherd of the flocks of Chuva.

But he was much more than an obedient son and shepherd.

Amongst the few treasures which his mother Naomi carried to the plains of Carmel was the sacred book of the law of the Jews, the chronicles of their judges and kings, the history of their wars, and the songs of their prophets.

All these she read to him, and taught him also to read.

Until the evening stars threw the shadows of things on the earth, and until the moon lighted the temple of the angels, she, on the roof of their house, where they slept, taught him this book.

And when he closed his eyes under the firmament, the firmament descended to him and enfolded him, until the rising sun raised it again high above him, and opened his eyes to the day.

They who have never slept in the open air under an eastern sky, secure on the housetop, can form no conception of the influence which

such repose exercises on the mind. We
Romans, who sleep under roofs and canopies
made by man, have mock purple and mock
stars for our envelopment; rich, gorgeous,
costly, but poor, poor imitations of the curtains and stars which enveloped the sleeping
shepherd boy Akiba, listening to his mother's
stories, until every story was a true event in
which he seemed to have taken part.

He was David, a shepherd standing before a
giant with a sling and a stone ; he was Solomon,
a wise king serving out justice from his throne.

In time this shepherd boy loved the book
of books beyond all else except his father, his
mother, and the sheep and lambs of the fold.
He knew not only every chronicle, proverb
and legend, but every passage, every word,
every letter. Of all the great scholars of the
scriptures of old not one was more learned,
than this shepherd of the plain, in the written
word.

Yet all this knowledge might have been
buried with him amongst his flocks had not a
strange event in his life changed the direction
of his feet.

As he grew into manhood, with the volume

of wonders a living part of his wonderful
nature, his heart began to yearn that he might
do some great deed, fight for some great cause,
remove some great wrong, build some great
city or temple, preach some great faith, teach
some great knowledge.

How were his wishes to be fulfilled?

Alas, he knew not. Except at stray times
when the rude merchants of the desert came
to carry off the wool that had been sheared
from the flock, or to buy the flocks that had
been reared for sale and drive them away, he
knew none with whom to speak. And these
men he shrank from; for too often they bore
from him some lamb from the fold that he had
tended, and loved, and cherished, and at whose
last look his heart would almost break.

At length the fate that always comes to
those of faith, who wait, came to him.

It was one of those days in the year
when on the plain day and night are all but
one; when the sun gives short pause from the
earth and in his absence leaves a trail of light
behind which, aided by that from the stars, is
caught up by the eastern glow that tells of his
return.

Akiba had gently cradled his flock, and returned to the home of his father Joseph and his mother Naomi, with his mind full of an ancient scripture ; a prophecy of one Balaam, a seer of the bygone ages :—

> 'Which saw the vision of the Almighty,
> Falling into a trance but having his eyes open.
> I shall see him, but not now ;
> I shall behold him, but not nigh ;
> There shall come a star out of Jacob
> And a sceptre shall rise out of Israel,
> And shall smite the armies of Moab,
> And destroy all the children of Sheth.
> And Edom shall be a possession,
> Sier also shall be a possession for his enemies,
> And Israel shall do valiantly.'

The shepherd boy slept on these thoughts, and next morning woke with them again on his mind.

He rose from his couch, offered up his morning prayer, listened for the tinkling of the bells which told him that the fold was astir, and leaving his parents still asleep descended from the housetop and straightway proceeded to the nearest fold.

As he traversed the plain towards this fold his practised and powerful eye caught sight of something in the extreme distance which was new to him entirely. It was, he thought, a moving train of living beings in gorgeous apparel, in the centre of which was an object like a sun, so bright was it and so shining, and from it there seemed to issue filmlike rays of rainbow colours.

Then he stood transfixed, wondering whether he should follow this light in its course; but while he wondered the gorgeous train and the star dissolved gradually away; dissolved itself into the sky, and ascended to its own divine sphere.

Filled with wonder, Akiba, after the vision had passed, hastened to the fold to find his surprise still further increased.

His flock was there as he had left it on the preceding night: he counted it, and the number was correct. The older members of the flock were moving about, preparing to be let out to go to the fresh grass by the side of the peaceful waters, and the little lambs, in groups where their mothers had left them, were playing their morning gambols according to their wont.

But now a new sight met him. In the gateway of the fence lay a little round heap covered with a robe of rich crimson dye fringed with a colour that glowed like the bright sun, as if the sun itself had imparted to it a portion of his own substance.

It was a Tyrian robe of silk, embroidered in its centre with a mystical sign and fringed with golden coloured threads, a shawl or coverlet, nothing more; but to Akiba, who had ever been content with his coat of clean sheepskin and knew no more of silk and gold than he had read of in the history of Solomon the wise king, it was a revelation.

He opened the gate of the fold, and raising the shawl discovered beneath it, sleeping like a lamb folded in it, a child, a boy child, clothed in pure white linen and enveloped also in a robe or mantle of purple with one bright golden gem shining from his breast.

In his astonishment Akiba raised his eyes from the little sleeper into the space of sky above, and once more in the extreme distance, but now high in the firmament, there beamed forth the bright light he had seen in the midst of the shining train, the rays from which fell down on to the breast of the boy child, and again dissolved away.

Oh, richness of prophecy! What the prophet had foretold had come to pass, and he, Akiba the chosen one, lived to declare it:

'I shall see him, but not now :
I shall behold him, but not nigh.'

Ages had come and gone and the words were fulfilled. The prophet had seen the one he predicted, but not in his mortal course : he had beheld him from that majestic train of spirits, but not nigh.

It was destined for this shepherd of the plain first to discover the star of Jacob and leader of Israel.

Henceforth, simple shepherd, think not of thyself, but learn and labour to raise thy people and exalt the star of thy people to its pre-ordained glory.

To him, Akiba, the fulfilment of the prophecy was revealed.

His emotion led him for a time away from himself. Then his reason intervened.

' What,' it said, ' what, deluded simpleton, dost thou mean by this ecstasy? Seest thou not that this is a specimen of human flesh and blood left by some travellers who wish to conceal it, lose it, forget it, and yet save it from death. Look thou under that boy child's shoulder, is there not a pouch stuffed with money? Seize thou that, it is thine, and thou art wealthy as Chuva thy master, for lo! upon it is written in thine own language:—"For the finder of the treasure."'

And so it was; there was money of great value. And notwithstanding his emotion Akiba, with the true instinct of his race, put the whole of it into the pouch of his garment.

Also, still influenced by his reasoning power, he went out of the fold to try and trace on the ground any sign of foot or wheel that should tell of human action, in explanation of the mystery. Either he was blind to such indications, or the winds had wafted them all away, and although in breathless haste he scanned the plain to look for footprints or signs of wheels, he found none.

As an eagle scans the earth and sky, Akiba scanned the plain, but he saw no further sign.

He returned to the fold to find his flock now all astir and waiting the guidance of their gentle master to be led forth for the day. He let forth the older ones according to his custom, retaining as hostages the lambs, whom their mothers had fed and to whom they would certainly return.

This duty done, Akiba had time to attend to the human lamb that had so mysteriously dropt into his fold. It was awake now, and gambolling like its four-legged companions in their early hours of play, for it was just old enough to run, with little falls now and again.

When Akiba came to the child and picked up the shawl that had covered it, it clung round his legs and tried to hide itself in the folds, laughing as children of health always laugh after a night of pure and wholesome sleep, a laugh that is all joy and gladness, like the young day itself.

In the heart of the shepherd, a heart as artless as the heart of his foundling, fondness soon took the place of amazement. He sat down on the shawl, rolled himself up in it to hide himself, pulled the child under it as the little thing dragged it off him, fondled him with tenderest embraces, kissed his sweet lips as he hung round his neck, hugged him, and rocked him to and fro until he was giddy with the exercise.

Suddenly the child set up a baby cry, the meaning of which Akiba had learned from his lambs. He knew what was asked for, and words he well remembered came into his mind :—

> ' When the young ones cry unto God
> They wander for lack of meat.'

He carried the little one tenderly to the house of his father and mother. He showed them the treasure he had found and the robes of purple and gold, and their hearts were filled with joy.

He would now have left the desert, but Joseph his father and Naomi his mother had pledged themselves there to remain, and their word must be their bond. So carefully concealing his wealth, he remained with them in the desert of Carmel, tending the flocks of Chuva, and watching over the new addition to his flock which had been so mysteriously added to his care, until his parents were numbered with their fathers.

After this event had occurred the work of Akiba as a shepherd was over. He was under no obligation to remain away from the haunts of men, and he pined to gain knowledge of all men and of all things. When, therefore, the steward of the merchant of Jerusalem next came to him, he resigned the stewardship of the flock, and with many tears left the home of his birth and early years, so soon as a successor appeared to relieve him of his duty.

Accompanied by his foundling boy, and carrying with him the rich treasure he had discovered and which he scorned to touch, he set forth for Cæsarea, on the borders of the great sea, of which city he had heard most as the abode of mankind.

They travelled short distances each day, and coming at length into little villages and hamlets Akiba found his knowledge of the Jewish scriptures of the greatest value. The people heard his reading of the scriptures with a delight they had never before experienced. To them the inspired words had been repeated in the worn-out voices of the synagogue, in one monotonous tone, with an assumed air of authority and with lifeless breath.

Now, they listened to the living word flowing to them as a river of life moved by a tongue of fire. The words from his lips had a new meaning, as of one from the wilderness declaring the way of the Lord.

He spoke to them through the prophet Micah, until they trembled as if the prophet were in very deed and truth before them. They asked him for explanations, and the lesson came from him as a natural product of mind. In many places they would have held him for life.

And in every place they called him Rabbi, offering him food at their tables and preparing for him and his the choicest raiment.

Reflecting on these tokens of recognition and affection, and accepting them as the declared signs of a great mission, Akiba conceived that he beheld still greater signs in the boy whom he had nurtured. For to this boy, when he was set up to read a chapter of the law or of the prophets, the multitude listened with a hushed wonder, which to Akiba was full of meaning.

The wonder was due to the fact that one so young could read so well, and the success depended really on the skill of the master who had taught so well. But the master had no such belief in himself. He was merely the instrument, the forerunner. He might be the chosen of Israel; this boy was the chosen of the chosen.

The boy himself, as he grew in strength, grew in will and resolution, but it was the will and resolution of his master, not his own. Akiba moulded him as a potter moulds the vessel; and filling him as far as he could be filled with his own exalted nature and hope, constructed for himself an idol at the feet of which he soon commenced to worship.

'My maidens,' interposed Lucilla at this point, 'when they hear this part of the story commence sometimes to blame the great Akiba. I tell them, Nay, blame him not, but let his action be a guide to you. You set up your idols. Is it not sweet if one of you have composed a song to hear another sing it; or if one has worked a tapestry for another to wish to possess it. If one hath built a house is it not music to hear another praise it; if one has made a name is it not the crown of joy that sons shall carry it on from generation to generation?'

'Truly, sweet lady, we will find no fault

with thy defence of Akiba,' replied the absorbed Fortunatus, ' but I yearn to hear the progress of the story.'

The boy—continued Marah in her reading —fed by Akiba with mental as well as bodily food, became more and more like to him, except that his talents were all reflected, and that whatever Akiba told him even of himself he absolutely believed.

So when Akiba said to him, 'Child of the desert, Simeon by name, thou shalt not die until thy mission be fulfilled, for no man can kill thee,' Simeon accepted the statement with such perfect faith that he tempted death and confirmed himself in the belief.

That he was born for some grand purpose he now knew, and if, like the Elijah of whom he had read, he were to see a chariot of fire ready to take him to heaven, he would not be afraid, but would enter the chariot as if it were his own.

At last they reached the borders of the great sea and came to Cæsarea.

To the shepherd of the plain the grandeur of this little place was a marvel. It dazed his sight, but with its wickedness his heart was wounded, and with the tyranny of its rulers, at that time under Trajan, his soul was set on fire. His impulse was to do as it was written by his favourite prophet :—

' Arise ye and depart, for this is not your rest ;
Because it is polluted it shall destroy you :
Even with a sore destruction.'

Notwithstanding this remonstrance, which seemed to him almost a command, he waited in Cæsarea for some time, and founded there a school where many scholars came, and where Simeon under his ever-watchful eye was taught all that he could learn. The lad grew in beauty, and in feats of strength and skill had no equal in all the city ; he kept also his own counsel.

So matters progressed well with Akiba ; his school flourished, he stood guileless and strong. The child placed under his guidance was good, and assisted by one of his people, Elkanah by name, whom he had taken into his school as a teacher and master, Akiba pursued his course in peace. He had found rest that was pleasant, labour that was useful. Was it all to last ?

The God of his fathers ordained it otherwise according to his divine will. Akiba had
a call, and leaving his school and his child of
the desert to the care of the faithful Elkanah,
he one day went down to Jerusalem.

AKIBA THE VANQUISHED.

Our story takes now a new line. It tells
of a man who has found a new master.

Akiba went down to the Holy City with
conceptions built on the readings of his child-
hood. The conceptions filled him with rapture ; the reality smote him to the heart.

He raised his hands in despair.

Is this Jerusalem?

Where are the gardens, the vineyards, the
mountains of olives, the streets of gold his
ardent youth had pictured?

Where are the holy places? Where is the
Temple? Where is the Ark of the Covenant,
and the Sanctuary?

Where are the people who walk in right-
eousness ; the rulers who sit at the gates
giving judgment ; where are they whose feet
are beautiful upon the mountains, who bring
good tidings and good will to men?

All day, all night, sleepless, hopeless, fast-
ing, restless, this disappointed child of Israel
traversed the city of his glorious dreams, to
find not one trace of all that he had believed
concerning it.

As the second evening fell he laid himself
down from pure fatigue, to rest at the foot of
a rising ground called Olivet. And he slept,
feeling that all his life had been filled by a
vain thing.

Jerusalem, the Holy City, was not his
Jerusalem. It was morally dead, but not
buried; with foul wounds of sin, and poison-
ous to the soul.

The morning sun roused him back to life.
He rose from the ground, and obtaining a few
olives and a roll of bread from one of the
wretched sellers of food who had come forth
in tattered garments, he fed and returned to
his work of observation.

A more certain enquiry assured him that
he was truly in Jerusalem.

The house of the Roman governor was now
the chief house of the city. The Roman
sentinels guarded the dead place as disciplined
mercenaries paid for the duty. Romans and

Greeks were there, and Jews in abundance: men, women and children, who bought, sold, and wrangled with Ethiops, Gauls, and other strangers, all commingled and equally at home.

He sought for a synagogue, and found it, but in seeking it found, also, the Roman temple, the church of the Galileans, the school of the unbelieving Stoics.

Think on it, think on it: false gods, false faiths, false schools in the city of David and Solomon!

He passed through a part of the city where the ruins left by the soldiers of Vespasian and Titus were still visible, although many years had passed away. Beneath the walls he came to a place where some Jewish women bewailed each day the departed glories, and his heart, if not his voice, went with them; his grief and shame were deeper even than theirs.

Distributing to these wailers some alms, he passed on. Wearied, footsore, broken in spirit, with bleeding soul, he passed on, feeling that to die with the city of his life were the happiest fate that could befall him.

He woke up from the desolation to catch a sound of something that rang sweetly, like music. He found that he had wound his way, without perceiving the fact, out of the ruined city into a highway, once the highway of princes, and still, as it appeared to him, wishing to be deceived, something beautiful, a place of fine houses and palaces.

The noise increased; a noise of the feet of horses and of tinkling bells; and soon all that made it was in sight, a sight the like of which he had never seen before.

A jet black horse richly harnessed, carrying silver bells, and stepping proudly, as knowing that he carried some one of distinction, led the way.

Around, and running by its side, was a troop of slaves gorgeously dressed, and hailing and shouting as they turned their faces to the rider of the horse, raised their fans of palm-leaves, and in every gesture and exultation testified their real or affected delight.

Their delight might indeed be real, for such a face as that which beamed back upon them were a joy to behold.

The face of a woman just within the lines

of womanhood, and animated with all the fire
of youthful beauty.

Her dress was simple, but rich and flowing.
Her outer robe, enveloping her loosely, fell
gracefully to her feet which, clad in sandals
of ivory, held by straps of purple velvet that
enlaced her ankles and ended in tassels of
gold, rested in a pair of bright stirrups, the
left foot a little lower than the right.   Over
her shoulders was cast a Tyrian mantle of rich
azure blue, worn cornerwise, so that while
one corner draped each arm, a third fell on
the back of the horse, and the fourth, looped
up, hung over her forehead, permitting to fall
on each side the rich lustrous tresses of her
dark brown hair, through which her ears, like
shells of pearl bearing pendants of diamonds,
peered forth.

Her dark and long arched eyebrows over-
hung eyes that were like light itself, so bright,
shadowless, and happy ; for the rest, a gentle
Jewish countenance, supported by an exquisite
neck, encircled by a kerchief of woven silver
tied in a bow which rested on her bosom.

Her arms and hands were free of all en-
cumbrances save a bracelet of pure mal-

leable gold, so malleable that it encircled her right arm from the wrist to the elbow in a serpentine line. The bracelet was the most significant of all her splendour. It was a present that had gained for her a name amongst the women of Jerusalem which some disdained, but which all envied.

A greater seeming contrast than she and the scholar Akiba could not have been found in all the earth. She all bright and fresh as the morning; he all worn, dusty, oppressed with sorrow, and weary as the night.

Her countenance fell as she gazed on the scholar and searcher after wisdom.

In listening to the stories which had been related to her about the destruction of Jerusalem, this child of the place had heard of one Jesus the son of Ananas, who for a long time before the memorable siege had traversed the city crying an awful cry, and had continued that cry during the siege until, while uttering it, a stone from a Roman catapult struck him amongst the voiceless dead around him. Was this man, this picture of woe before her, the same son of Ananas restored to life? Would he begin to cry that bitter cry, 'A voice from the east, a voice from the west, a voice from the north, a voice from the south, a voice from the four corners of the earth crying Woe! woe! woe! to Jerusalem'?

Strangest of strange coincidences, Akiba had been seized at the moment with an overpowering impulse to repeat the very words. The story was also on his mind, and he had echoed it but for the sight before him.

What she, the rich child of Jerusalem, expected him to say she herself stopped by her mere presence, through a rapid diversion of his thoughts.

She checked the movements of her steed, and her chain of slaves stood still.

For a moment she averted her head to the left side from him who stood on her right, and holding the white reins in her left hand put her right hand back towards the pouch suspended to the saddle as if feeling for some coins to give, through one of her slaves, to a mendicant. Then she hastily repented the act, regained the hold of the reins in her right hand, coloured a deep crimson in the face, and met the flashing gleam of the scholar with a

return shaft keen as an arrow-point, and so
well aimed as to pierce his inmost soul.

A moment more and she rode on, pushing
her steed into a quicker pace, and stooping
down to the chief of her slaves as they got
out of hearing from the stranger, she asked,
with an emotion she could not altogether sup-
press :—

'Who, Justus, who is that man?' But
Justus, the chief slave, knew not, neither did
any of his band.

'See,' replied she, with a voice of authority
never to be questioned. 'See that by nightfall
all that can be told of that man be brought
to me.'

'Your slaves will lay it at your feet,' and,
without a moment's loss of time, the trustiest
of the band, after a word from Justus, was
receiving his orders to depart into the city.

'It is well,' was the response. 'See to it
thoroughly.'

She rode on, but never before in so strange
an ecstasy. Now she paced until the slaves
were breathless; suddenly she stopped, so
abruptly as to pull her horse back into
the breasts of the slaves who ran behind

her, driving them backwards many feet; then, as suddenly, she turned round and in deep meditation made her way to her own house.

Surely, thought the slaves, our mistress hath been be-spirited by that strange man. And the slaves were wise.

The strange man, himself even more be-spirited, stood rooted to the spot where the vision had stopped his exclamations. Breathless, speechless, sightless, he stood there so stricken he was glad of the help of a poor man, to whom the day before he had given alms, to lead him to an inn.

'Who,' he gasped in Hebrew, as his senses and powers of speech returned, 'who, good friend of mine in hour of need, who is she who with her slaves passed us by?'

'She, my son,' replied the kindly guide in the same tongue, 'she, my son, is the last remaining link of the royal house of Sala, an ancestor of our father David. She is the golden serpent of Jerusalem, the only child of Chuva, the Princess Tyra. Beware, my son, of the Princess Tyra the daughter of Chuva.'

Vain words! as well tell a man about to
be crucified to beware of the cross.

Their eyes had met and their souls had
mingled.

'Love mingles through the eyes, and soul
meets soul there; my Servien spoke fine
words, but it was his eyes won me,' once more
interposed Lucilla.

'Happy Servien,' smiled out Fortunatus,
'but pray thee go on with Akiba and the
golden serpent.'

'Me thinks, wise Roman, thou hast fallen
in love with the mere description of the serpent of Jerusalem.'

'I plead guilty, that I may hear still more.'

Their eyes had met, continued the reader,
and he had been stricken. Nor was he the
first that had been so wounded. The princess
Tyra of the royal house of Sala had gained
a reputation, that had gone far and wide, for
her prowess and skill in vanquishment.

The Roman officers at their banquets
drank to her name, the Greek merchants
bought choice jewels far away, the memory
of her the cause of the purchase; the Jewish
youths looked with envy on the invaders who

sought her hand, some for her wealth and all for her beauty.

She herself, unconscious of it as it seemed to those about her, lived on untouched by the daily adoration. Against her fair fame not one spoke a word. The old and poor Jews said she was the golden serpent, not in blame of her, but as indicating that she was too wise to be caught by the allurements before her. They loved her to their hearts' core, and well they might, for she had no pleasure so great as that of distributing to them the wealth of her house. Her slaves knew every living face in Jerusalem, and amongst the Jews every house, so that if want entered a Jewish house, a bearer of good tidings from the princess was sure to meet it with befitting aid.

'I would rather,' said the Roman Governor of Jerusalem, 'be at peace with the Princess Tyra than have another legion of soldiers, for she holds the keys of the city.'

Once from the Emperor himself his lieutenant received a necklace to give to an ally so courted. She dared not refuse acceptance of the gift, but in an hour, dismantled and unrecognisable, it was on its way to Damascus for sale, in separate parts, for the people of her blood.

Her ride in the morning on which she met Akiba was on a mission of goodness. She was about to visit the oldest representative of the House of Judah, whose end by length of days was near, and towards whom she felt it a duty of respect and dignity to proceed in princely train.

The visit was one of the visits of her life, never forgotten, never put off, never stopped until this day, when to the astonishment of all her people she returned without making it, and entering her house straightway sought her chamber. The astonishment of her women folk was the more increased when they were told that the return was caused by the sight of a stranger to Jerusalem.

'She has seen,' they whispered in their mystical mode of thought, 'she has seen the face of Israel.'

The excitement calmed down, the slaves dispersed themselves to their various tasks; the attendants resumed their quiet watchings, but the Princess re-appeared not, and for many hours the mansion was as silent as a gorgeous sepulchre. As if afraid to awaken some slumbering much beloved sick one, the inmates moved silent of foot, and spoke to each other in whispers, ready at any moment to obey the commands of their mistress, yet not daring to approach beyond the vestibule leading to her apartments, at the door of which the faithful Justus reclined and would have remained until he died had the service been required of him.

As the evening approached the Princess re-appeared amongst her people. But how changed!

Her dress, of the purest white, was divested of every ornament she had been most pleased to wear. Her voice carried with it a subdued gentleness and sweetness ; her graces of manner, modified by some sweet sadness, were entrancing ; her expression formerly commanding, however gentle, was now of seraphic beauty, so that they who conversed with her said to each other, that she must have been admitted into the company of the heavenly host and have learned of them.

To some extent these faithful observers

were right in their conjecture. The Princess Tyra, in the hours of her seclusion, had been in transporting reverie, according to her belief, with the seraphic host.

She too had received her call.

The face of Akiba had filled her with wonder. It filled her soul.

It was a face she had expected to see, and yet she could recall no one particular moment of the expectation. It must have been the face of Israel!

She cast herself on the couch in the quiet room where she was wont to muse, to read, to sleep.

How long she remained there she knew not at the time.

A moment, an hour, a day, a year, an age, ages of ages!

She knew not.

But this she knew, that however long it was she rose with the cry:—

'Oh that I might thus live on for ever.'

Her reverie was the picture of things unseen, a revelation as clear as was ever made to human mind; for to her doubts and philosophic questionings were as follies which the

unbelievers believe in their heads and dis-
believe in their hearts. To her primitive faith
God spoke and it was done ; the sea was His
and He made it, and His hand formed the
dry land. He robed Himself in light as with
a garment, and by His angel or His angels,
not by Himself, for He is a spirit, but by them
as intermediaries between His spirit and mortal
flesh, He had revealed himself even to her,
Tyra, the daughter of Chuva and his wife, the
princess of the royal house of Sala.

In that sweet revelation she beheld herself
clothed in white robes standing in what had
been once the Temple of Solomon in all its
glory. In some way, escorted by an angel
visible alone to her, she was in the train of
that great king at the time when, with an
invocation matchless in its poetic fervour, he
opened the house that he had built. She heard
the very words of the king.

The sounds of the voice died away, and she
was alone in the temple. The king, the court,
the musicians, the priests, the servitors were
gone ; the light of day was gone ; the angel
was gone ; but she remained.

In that solemn silence, though she felt not

mortal pain, she knew that she was cold and
by that sense was almost roused to common
life, a fact she afterwards remembered and
which confirmed her faith. It was a passing
moment of terror lest He whom the heaven of
heavens cannot contain should in very deed
appear, and she be consumed by the glory of
His presence.

The terror passed away and was forgotten
in the event which succeeded. In the moment
of her alarm the blue veil of the temple before
which she stood melted into an imperial sky.
The Holy of holies became the firmament;
the ark was resolved into a cluster of glorious
stars, and the cherubim that guarded it moved
into the mighty space; the voices of unseen
thousands filled the air with song; and a
fragrant incense, communicating an ethereal
delight, completed the supreme pleasure of
existence in that new temple in which she,
alone, of all mortals, stood!

Surely one of the angels of light will
speak to her. Surely some voice from the
hosts of the blessed will tell this child of
the earth why she is called and what she is
to do.

No, she is not called by an angel.   But
yet is she none the less called.

The majesty of the vision is subdued,
folded as it were into human dimensions. She
is in the temple built with hands once more,
the veil is still raised, the Holy of Holies is
open to her favoured view, the cherubim
spread out their wings over the ark of the
covenant, a heavenly light glows, and before
the ark, clothed in the robes of the high
priest of Israel and prince of his people, is the
stranger, the man stricken with woe whom she
had met wandering in the street of the city.

In adoration he turns his face to the ark.
He bends as if under the weight of a load
heavier than he can bear. He will fall!
She rushes to save him, but the veil of the
temple descends between them, and with the
cry of joy of which we have already heard,
she is restored to common life and its common
realities.

'Truly, sweet lady, I will confide to thee
all the love stories of my history,' murmurs the
delighted Fortunatus, as Marah for a moment
rested from her narrative, 'that thou mayest
embalm them in such choice setting. I will

be sent down to posterity by thee, a perfect
memory of love, in a sarcophagus of fancy
and a pyramid of fame.   Now I presume, in
my earthly fashion, they are going to be
married and for ever happy.'

'Anticipate not too rashly, Oh hard philosopher,' resumed Lucilla. 'But Marah must
read on.'

In time the news was spread abroad
that the golden serpent of Jerusalem had been
charmed and won by the eyes of a poor Rabbi
named Akiba, once the shepherd servant of
Chuva her father. 'And it is as it should be,'
said the wiser men of the city, 'since beauty
and wealth are the best friends of wisdom
and knowledge.'

'When the Princess Tyra gives up her rule
in Jerusalem Cæsar must send me another
legion,' said the Governor of Jerusalem.

'What an ancient fool was I to sacrifice
all my little store to buy a bracelet for that
golden serpent!' sighed Damos the Greek
merchant, who with his native craft believed
that the way to win a woman's love was to
bedeck her with rich jewels.

And hundreds of poor hearts throbbed
with fear lest their homes should lose the

light of her countenance and the generosity of her hand.

And her attendants and slaves whispered to each other, ' When shall we have another home like this in the house of our dearest mistress and friend ? '

With it all there was rejoicing, for the news of marriage is always the hope of a festival.

The sweet Tyra lived in hope, and Akiba the scholar waited in its embrace. For the moment all ambition, all effort of learning was lost in this blissful swiftly running tide of love.

Alas ! alas ! that such a tide should receive one moment of interruption.

Yet Fate ordained it, and so it was.

Chuva, the father of the happy maiden, was away in Tyre, from whence his wealth was derived. Never doubting his assent, the Princess, his only beloved child, despatched to him trusty messengers conveying the news of her love, the true history of her lover, the account of his great learning, wisdom, and goodness, the beauty of his person, and all else that a fond and spoiled maiden in pangs of love would, under such circumstances, say to an adoring parent.

Chuva, when he heard the news, accepted the message with a rage before unknown by his oldest friends. He sent back the messenger hastily with imprecations; in his great wrath bade the sweet princess leave his house forthwith and speak to him no more; made a new testament, leaving all his wealth away from her, and added to the document the blighting curse of his fathers on her and hers.

The princess received the news in despair. Then, recovering her fortitude, she clothed herself in mourning as for one dead, and sending for Akiba told him all, bidding him hold her, now no longer a princess but a poor daughter of Jerusalem, unworthy the love of one so great and learned and wise as he.

'Nay, my greater and dearer love,' exclaimed Akiba, 'be still mine own. Thy wealth, which I never wanted nor envied, is dross compared to thee. Be thou alone the wealth. Thy father's wealth is the sweeping of the streets; thou art the dust of the stars, and more than ever mine.'

What could the Princess Tyra do or say after such words?

As may be believed, she left her princely palace even with joy; consecrated with simplest

marriage vows her life to her beloved, followed him, cherished him, and day by day
was more and more enriched by the return of
his affection.

As a teacher Akiba could easily make his
way, so that the princess took not one precious
treasure from her father's house. As her dead
mother had left all in order, so she, disturbing
no single thing, tore herself from her weep-
ing maids and slaves, and forsaking all others
clung to her bosom lord.

They travelled and taught until they
reached Alexandria, the city of scholars, where
Philon Judæus had lived and written, and
where Jews were esteemed for their wisdom.

In Alexandria there was a grand synagogue in which, on days of worship, the men
sat apart according to their guilds; the gold-
smiths in their parts, the coppersmiths in theirs,
the joiners in theirs, the weavers in theirs;
for Jews always divide themselves into guilds,
and will do so through all time.

At the foot of all the guilds might be seen
those who waited for work, and there Akiba
took his seat.

In the centre the Reader, clad in white

vestments, bore the Sudarm, or flag with which
to give the great congregation the signal for
the ringing Alleluiah and the loud Amen.

Above all sat the seventy, the elders of the
people, on seats of gold.

And from her place on the women's side
the lovely Princess Tyra, the beholden of
all beholders, so ravishing was her beauty,
watched her husband sitting humbly at the
feet of the guilds waiting for honest work.

They asked him, when the worship was
over :—

' Who art thou and what is thy vocation,
and who is this woman thy wife ? '

It was a mere ceremony, for in truth the
whole story and the fame of Akiba and the
princess had preceded them.

Soon, very soon, Akiba became in Alexandria the most renowned teacher there;
learned above all others, and the central occupant of the golden seat of the synagogue.   So
do those that humble themselves become
exalted.

They tarried in Alexandria seven years
and then they returned to Jerusalem, for
Tyra still mourned for her father's love, and

having now a son hoped to win forgiveness, if not by her own persuasion by that of her child, who inherited her beauty of person and his father's intelligent mind.

Entering Jerusalem in the quietest manner and making themselves known to none of the people, Tyra with her son sought her father's house, and communicating her wishes to the faithful servants, whose love she had never lost, stood before Chuva, her sire, and placing her child also before him prayed his pity, his forgiveness, and his blessing.

It was a pleading one would have thought that no man could have resisted, and when the child raised his ruby lips, and put out his little hand, Chuva was indeed touched to the heart by both child and grandchild, for these were all the living wealth that he possessed.

But he was a Jew, and a Jew, it is declared, never forgives.

He sent them both from his presence, or rather he withdrew from them.   He left them in their tears and sobs on their knees, and entered the court of his house where strangers wait, meaning to take the air and recover his anger and cool his rebellious heart.

In the outer court of his house he found, to his surprise, a stranger of noble build, tall and motionless, before whose searching glance yet gentle expression he, Chuva, shook and trembled.

Stricken with the superstition common to worldly minds, the old man, in the suddenness of his wonder, believed that he was visited by some being of supernatural gifts and power.

'What asketh my lord of his servant?' gasped the affrighted merchant. 'Ask only and thou shalt have.'

'I ask for nothing,' replied the visitor, 'I come to claim my own. Akiba waits to remove from hate to love his wife and son.'

In Magnes there is said to be an earth or stone that draws to it or repels from it, as it wills, all of its kind that are near to it ; and amongst men there are they who have the power of that stone.

Akiba was a prince of the power, and Chuva was under his magical spell. Had he dared, Chuva would have thrown himself on the breast of his conqueror ; as it was, he fell at his feet, but, raised by the strong and loving arms that soon surrounded him, he very quickly discovered himself the centre of his three children, they the objects of his proud admiration, and he of their united love.

Chuva revoked the will he had made, left all his treasures to Akiba the wise, and therewith crowned the success of him who afterwards entered Paradise, and who is now the chief of his people, for though learning be ever so great, wealth well-spent will make it greater.

But, as it is written, ' Boast not thyself of to-morrow, for thou knowest not what a day may bring forth ;' so whilst Akiba and his son were away to visit Alexandria a plague struck the holy city, and when on his return he landed here at Joppa a messenger met him to tell him that both Chuva and the Princess Tyra were in the home of the departed, that their last breaths had carried his beloved name, and that their last hopes were that he would pray for them, that they might be set free from the prison where the souls of the dead, purified from their sins, are made fit for the kingdom of heaven.

We have a promise that when the gates

of heaven are shut to prayer they are open to tears, and in that promise Akiba found relief for his bursting heart. Then followed the prayer which the Romans know not, the prayer that is only Israel's weapon, a weapon tried in a thousand battles, a weapon inherited from the fathers of Israel.

And Akiba taught his little son that prayer which Israel ever repeats when the good die and the earth loses them :—

'*Blessed is the righteous judge.*'

To Jerusalem Akiba bent his way, to find his home still a house of mourning. But when he had performed all the rites of holiness and honour to his lost ones, he came back to Joppa as to the place of his call, that he might here obey the word, and find peace in his sorrow.

Honour the sons of the poor, for it is they who bring knowledge into glory.

And by these words Akiba lives to this hour.

'A strange, strange history,' observes Fortunatus as Marah's voice ceases. 'But what, I pray thee, was the fate of the foundling who brought Akiba his first treasure?'

' Ah, thereby hangs a mystery that even
Lucilla cannot solve, nor Akiba himself,' broke
in the matter-of-fact Servien, who having
finished his inspection had rejoined the listening group. ' When Akiba, after his tour of
love had ended, went with his wife to Cæsarea
to fetch the boy, in whose fate her woman's
heart was moved, it was not to be found. The
very house in which he had been left was
rased to the earth ; the school was no more,
All that could be learned was that a rather
sharp Jewish quarrel, in some way connected
with the synagogue, had arisen in Cæsarea ;
that some Jews of Jerusalem and some Jews
of Samaria had disputed for possession of the
synagogue ; that a Roman force had quelled
the disturbance, not without bloodshed, and
that when all was over, the master of the
school, connected with the place, who had
played a leading part in the disturbance as a
Jew of Galilee, and who more than once before
had made himself most objectionable and rebellious to the power of Cæsar, was crucified,
and that all who belonged to him had disappeared for ever.

' There is a rumour that Trajan himself,

who was at that time in Jerusalem, had some hand in this affair, for reasons more weighty than at first sight would appear. But this has now become an old wife's story, well-nigh forgotten or treated as fable.'

As the night is far advanced and Servien is weary, the friends separate for rest and sleep, and Fortunatus, with a courteous fare-well to his hostess and host, seeks his chamber.

Yet long after he is ensconced in that quiet retreat he recalls the story he has heard, for he was in Cæsarea when Trajan was at Jerusalem, and if some advice he then gave had been followed, many events which have been related in these pages, with many which have to follow, had never occurred, and this record of them had never been written.

So true it is that the smallest incidents of one age may extend through ages, and that there is nothing human, however little, that may not leave a permanent mark in the book of humanity.

CHAPTER XV

SCHOLARS AHEAD.

THE day following upon the recital of the history of Akiba the Wise by the wife of Servien, was rapidly passed by her exemplary husband in the company of his friend and visitor, the learned and accomplished Fortunatus, in inspecting the towers and places of strength of Joppa, the legion that was stationed there, the armoury, the weapons, the shipping, and the surrounding country.

Servien had now his history to tell; how Cestius the Roman general, during the time of the Jewish revolt in the reign of Nero, had taken Joppa by a combined movement on sea and land, had destroyed eight thousand of its people, and had laid the place waste; how it then became the centre or home of a piratical navy, which made the sea from Egypt to Tyre, and even across to the isles of Greece, dangerous, if not impassable; how Vespasian, in his time, sent a force which drove the pirates to their ships on the sea, out of the reach of the Roman darts; how 'a black north wind' forcing the pirates back upon the rocks, left them so much to the mercy of their enemies that they were destroyed by thousands, many falling upon their own swords, so that the sea was reddened for some miles with their blood; how Vespasian determined, upon this recapture of the place, to make it a strong Roman fortress or camp, and left there many horse-men and some foot, who laid bare the country all round about; and how, for a long period, the town remained nothing more than a soli-tary place of Roman soldiery.

But Servien had also a later story to tell. He told that the number of ships from the Great Sea still so continuously put in to Joppa that, in spite of Rome, it became once more a port or gateway to Jerusalem; that Greeks and Romans, as well as Jews, frequented it; that in time the Jews from Phœnicia and Egypt and other parts of the world settled there under Roman rule; that with their usual genius the Jews brought trade, money, and wealth to the spot, together with much learning and life ; and that, giving up all thoughts of war, they had turned the reconstructed place, mainly by the influence of Akiba, into a great school, to which over twelve thousand scholars resorted, to pass from it, by its ready exit, to the schools of Alexandria, Athens, and Rome itself, bearing forth their learning, and bringing back the learning of other peoples and lands.

'Thou art as great an enthusiast, my Servien, about these Judeans as thy wife,' observed Fortunatus, 'and, in truth, thou hast measured them correctly ; they are traders in wisdom as well as in money. But art thou sure about their loyalty? These weapons they forge for thee, hast thou confidence that thou art the only keeper of all that are made ?'

'Confident,' replied Servien. 'They make the weapons at Akiba's forges, not by multitudes of men working there, but by a very few students at a time, as a pastime of the schools, and under the eye always of our centurions, as thine own eyes shall witness.'

Not a bench, not a class, not a work, mental or physical, of the great school of

Akiba at Joppa escapes the observation of Fortunatus.

A poor soldier compared with Servien, he is a better soldier here. His tablets fill as he passes from one part to another. He will show the tablets to Cæsar; he will perhaps show them to the world, publish them if he shall live. His sentences are of necessity brief, but, as may be seen in the specimens below, are sufficient to help his memory, as so many rests for it, when he shall sit down in his study in his garden at Rome in sweet retirement.

EXCERPTS FROM THE NOTE-BOOK OF FORTUNATUS OF ROME RESPECTING JOPPA AND THE JEWS THERE IN THE REIGN OF THE EMPEROR HADRIAN.

' The common statement that there are twelve thousand scholars at Joppa under Akiba the Wise is less than the fact.

' There are two hundred youthful Jews in each class, and there are seventy-two classes, after their mystic number.

' The youths are all strong and thoughtful, they fill up half the day at their books, the rest in bodily exercises or manual labour.

' They march, and run, and obey words of command like men of war, but Servien wisely allows them no weapons, they may not even discharge a bow, though they themselves have made it.

' They write with a stylus half a cubit long, which

they carry in their girdles point upwards, so that it may be distinguished from a dagger. Why so long?

'They have remarkable skill in the manufacture of weapons. In every school there is a forge at which they make, each day, a sword, a bow, a javelin, and a spear, without interfering with the ordinary work of learning.

'They make armour also, helmets, breastplates, and chainwork, with fine skill.

'In an emergency they could equip a thousand soldiers a week.

'Servien only allows one class a day to make weapons, all of which weapons are removed as they are finished.

'Servien directed that one class should make before us a bow, a sword, a shield, and a javelin. Four sets of the youths were put to the task, seven to the bow, seven to the sword, seven to the shield, and seven to the javelin.

'These Jews do everything by sevens. Why?

'They sing in turns, during their work, some sacred song that bears on what they are doing.

'The youths we met sang sayings taken from their books as they worked, according to the labour. Thus:

'"Iron is taken from the earth.

'"Brass is melted out of stone.

'"Iron sharpeneth iron, and the face of a man that of his friend.

'"Og, king of Bashan, lo his bedstead was of iron; nine cubits long, and four cubits broad.

'"Thou shalt break them with a rod of iron."

'Then they sang some weird prophecy about a great king who saw a great image with feet of iron, that was smitten by a stone cut without hands. The image represented some kingdom which the stone should crush.

'The work proceeded with the singing. They gave to iron a spring, and a bow was wrought out of such iron, and a sword like the finest of the cast; the sword bent like the bow ; and a javelin, made for Servien, was cast by him full fifty footsteps, into a figure of wood shaped like a man.

'These youths obey their superiors like soldiers.

'They make the sun their fellow-workman.

'They build and furnish their own habitations, and earn their own bread.

' They are taught leech-craft and other useful callings, "because," say their fathers, " a man who fails to give his son a trade maketh him a rogue."

'Would that our Roman fathers believed and practised the same rule.

'They share equally each other's goods, and him that would be greatest amongst them they make the least, because their scripture tells them that a good name is choicer than riches ; that the rich man is wise in his own conceit ; but, that the poor man, who has understanding, finds him out.

'Would that our Roman youths were taught such wisdom.

'They are expert as fishermen.

'They make their own bread and raiment.

'They drink no wine.   Wine, they are told in one of their proverbs, is a mocker.

'They learn every tongue.

'They are sent forth to gain more knowledge.

And they worship day and night the God of their fathers, declaring boldly that He, one God, is alone to be worshipped.

'They abhor graven images, and will rather die than worship them.

'They obey the laws of Cæsar, but will not bow down nor burn incense before his image, because they say their God is a jealous God, and visits the sins of the fathers on the children to the third and fourth generation.

'Their God has no form, and no image of Him exists. Enquiring his name, they refuse to pronounce it because it is too sacred to be uttered. He, they say, is a spirit whom no one hath seen; but his angel or intermediator may communicate with man, and his own spirit fills man.

'They keep holy the seventh day of the week. They have daily prayers and services, each hour of the day being set apart for some particular service.

'These religious rites Servien is instructed by Cæsar not to interrupt, so the youths grow bold. They meet in their synagogues; they sing a sacred hymn; they read, in turn, lessons from their scriptures; they offer up prayers to their Creator; they chant psalms; they make responses; and they listen to their rabbis who preach to them from a tribune or from the altar. All this they are permitted to do, but one thing Servien will not allow them to do, because it would put them in possession of knives, axes, and other weapons: they may not offer up the bodies of animals to their deity, no, not even at festivals.

'But on festival days they are allowed to burn the fat of animals, as candles, with incense, at the altar, by which they raise a savoury and sweet odour with fire and smoke. A symbolical sacrifice for which they are grateful.

'The priest stands before the altar, wearing twelve jewels on his breast, and richly robed. The singers in white robes stand behind the priest before the altar. They all turn to the east when they pray, and they all kneel when the commandments of their early prophet are declared from the altar.

'Once yearly they hold a "passover," or religious feast in remembrance of their great deliverance from Egypt.

'Once yearly they have a day for atonement of

their sins, when they sit all day in the synagogue and confess their sins with many prayers, and count their prayers with beads, which they carry round their necks.

'Like the Egyptians, they bury their dead. Questioned as to the souls of their dead they are mysterious, but speak of some prison or place of purification, and say it is good for the living to pray for the deliverance of the dead from it.

'Pressed on the question whether they expect a new deliverer to arise amongst them as a Messiah, which is always laid to their charge, they answer invariably in the same significant words: "The Holy One of Israel is our law-giver, and Cæsar is Cæsar. The will of the Holy One be done on earth as it is in heaven."

'From the uniformity of this saying they must have been trained to declare it.

'Many of these questions and answers amused Servien, because he, who has married one of their blood, a wife to whom he is childishly devoted, thought I had met my masters in wisdom.

'I, Fortunatus, think so too; but it is Servien, and not I, who may find out the truth of it most speedily.

'One thing these Jews proved to me by their lives, that work of the limbs and work of the mind go well together, as Plato has taught in his book, the "Timæus."'

To the refined and observant Fortunatus, who had visited every part of the Roman world, these Jewish schools are in fact a model, and his praises of them are as warm as they are cautious and discreet. He determines that, if life be spared him, he will master these schools and their mysteries. What is the book of which in every school he hears so much? He questions Servien, who knows no more of it than the mere mechanical facts that seventy or seventy-two Jews, all considered as scholars of highest rank, are at work upon it under the chief, Akiba; and that to the thousands of youths in the schools it is a book the treasuring of which and the copying of which keeps them out of mischief towards Rome and his legion.

Fortunatus hears the words of Servien with all respect, but does not accept them as final.

Fortunatus has been a student of the stirring history of Babylon. He recalls how under a Babylonish captivity the Jews ceased to be a savage and learned to be a wise and cultured race, yearning still for home yet loving their enlightened captivity. He has heard that when they returned from their captivity and reentered into possession of their promised land, they were not the Jews of old, but that their mind was set on a new reading, interpretation, and preservation of their ancient and sacred records. And now, with their new order of thought, he discovers them re-editing, so to speak, the book of the Word, the Book of the world, the book of Truth.

Would that he, a born son of nature, a philosopher, could join in the labour.

Servien is much amused at his absorption in such nonsense.

'Ah, my Servien, keep thou these Jews in their place under Cæsar, watch them with an eye as vigilant as that of an eagle waiting for its prey, for they, from their earliest times, have been taught of the serpent, and creep noiselessly at your feet until they grip you. They have the art of charming you by their gentleness and beating you by their subtlety. Be ever on thy guard, but say not one word against their sacred writings and treasures of wisdom, for in them is the secret of everlasting knowledge and wisdom.'

'My wife, whom I have named Lucilla,' muses Servien, ' says these same sayings, which is not strange, seeing that she is born of this people. But that a learned Roman should repeat her words is, like the very books of these Jews, a mystery. I care not to fathom it. If the worst come to the worst, I will make short work of it. I will burn every rag of a

book that Cæsar may reign, Lucilla and Fortunatus notwithstanding.'

With curious insight Fortunatus reads the
mind of his honest and resolute friend.

'Thou thinkest, Servien, if the books of
these Jews led to revolt what a fire they would
make at thy bidding?'

'My very thoughts.'

'Thou art bold, Servien, but this were
beyond thy power. Amidst thunders and light-
nings which our Jove himself could not raise,
the first of those books came to these Jews.
Their God spoke to them His own commandments. I know the story, and the name of the
Jew who wrote the words on tablets of stone.
What one of the masters pronounced in the first
school I understood, and why the scholars bent
so low when he added:

'"Fear God and keep his commandments."
"And do not unto another what thou wouldst
not have another do to thee."

'Those are open sayings, old and true,
which their sages have taught, but they have
others more secret, and that have most to do
with thee. Jerusalem, they say, was won by
Vespasian because the young were not taught.

The world is saved by the breath of the young. These are the lessons of the schools we have visited, and though thou burn all their books, my noble Roman, they will rise again.'

And thus in friendly controversy the two sworn friends, so different in nature, the one root and branch a soldier, the other root and branch a scholar, spent their day, surveying Joppa, its schools, its forts, its streets, its bazaars, its quays, its ships, its peoples of Greeks, Romans, Jews, Egyptians, Tyrians.

All the world of Joppa and its inevitable wife.

Leaving them so occupied, let us, by a return flight to Britain, re-seek our heroes there, and firstly him who, to please a Roman mob, ran for his life as a pillar of fire, and was saved from the burning.

CHAPTER XVI.

IN HAPPY FLIGHT.

SIMEON and his two friends, the handsome chieftain and his lovely child, made quick footsteps over another ascent, which leads them still farther from the Roman camp ; and here the wise guide once more takes counsel of himself.

Some wild and cruel rollickers from the camp may follow us, he argues, or even a number of armed men may follow us, and seizing us take us back into the furious claws of the enemy from which we have escaped !

To Simeon these apprehensions are as so much idle wind. He has retained beneath the sackcloth in which he had been enveloped his trusty sword or falchion, and woe to a dozen rollickers or others who come beneath its swing. Moreover, he who has already

escaped such great dangers will escape all.
Such is his destiny.

The Philosopher listens and marvels; but
learning soon, with practised skill, the mind
and character of this singular youth he proceeds to influence him in the only way in
which he is open to reason.

It is a circumstance as curious as it is
natural both to him and to his child, whom
he calls by the name of Erine Leoline, that
this youth whom they have so far saved is
now dedicated to their solemn charge. It is
a feeling which all who have once befriended
him feel ever afterwards. That also is his fate.

His new mentor quickly reading his character, proceeds to act upon him rapidly and
effectively; and soon the stubborn nature is
subdued by so wise and gentle a counsellor.

'Thou art here, good Simeon,' he answers,
' for such thou tellest me is thy name; thou art
here and the Mighty One whom thou servest
has need of thee; but wisdom must temper
courage, and what fate thinkest thou will
befall thine unhappy friends should Roman
hands fall upon us? Thou mayest be under
divine protection, we are certainly not so

favoured. Thinkest thou this child of mine, so frail, so fair, will escape their penalties and their pleasure?'

The words are enough.

'The God of my fathers hath given me over to thy safe keeping,' was his reply: 'henceforth thou shalt do with me as thou desirest. I will call thee Leon, and will obey thee as if I were another child of thine.'

'Thou art wise, my son, as thou art bold. They who sought thy life do not mean thee to escape. They wait only to drink wine ere they pursue thee. Thou hast refused to offer up incense to their king, thou art an arrow in the side of their second king or Governor, and they are too strong even for thee when force alone is master. We, therefore, will try the wisdom thou dost not despise.'

They are now on a plain, proceeding as swiftly as their feet can carry them, one on each side of him whom we with Simeon shall henceforth call Leon. So led they proceed towards the west guided by the reading of the stars, until they come to a deserted native hut or rather considerable size, with other smaller huts, equally deserted, clustered near to it.

It is a hut made of earth and poles and straw. Into the earth a large scoop or opening has once been cut; the earth has been thrown up on all sides, except the southern side, facing the sun, to form a wall or bank; into the bank poles have been planted so as to meet in a point at the centre; around these poles stubble or thatch has been attached to make a roof; within the hut at the farthest extremity from the sloping southern entrance a hearthstone has been erected, and therewith the home of the native Briton has been made complete.

The combination of huts formed once a native village. It was the seat of a chief, and was surrounded altogether by an enbankment of earth.

Some years ago it was the scene of a great fight; the Roman soldiers on their march through the country westward came upon it, met with a resistance altogether unexpected, and in revenge, when they became victors, slew every man, woman, and child of the place, leaving the dead to bury the dead.

In that village of desolation no one ever afterwards dwells.

It is a haunted desolation. Roman and
Briton alike view it, from the distance, with
equal superstition and fear.

Fortunately it has not escaped the notice
of the observant Leon. He passed it but a
day or two ago, went into it alone ; read in the
remains he found there its history, and now
again approaches it as a trap laid for his pursuers should they follow in his wake.

Nature has been more bountiful than man
to this unfortunate nest of death ; she has
wept over it with her genial showers, and her
wild briars and dog roses have covered it in
so as finally to bury it in beauty. Here the
birds build their nests, and here the dead leaves
of the plain, wafted to the spot, cover up the
skeletons of the slaughtered men, women, and
babes.

Leon has surveyed the place, and has
gratefully thanked the supreme power he
worships that no such nest of desolation
could be found in all his own peaceful land.

He brings his companions to a rest here
while he explains to them his design.

Breaking through the long grass which
obstructs the entrance to the chief hut, and

lighting his way with a luminous point which he has struck from a kind of rod carried in a wallet, by his side he comes upon what he expected, the bones of one of the victims of the fray. There are few of them, for wild beasts have carried many away, but what remain are sufficient for his purpose.

With quick and precise skill he spreads out quickly at the entrance of the hut a bed of leaves, loose wood, and thatch torn from the slanting and decaying roof; and, on this bed he lays the bones in natural order, as if a man making for the interior of the hut had fallen down headlong at the entrance.

Returning now to Simeon whom he has left a little distance off, he removes from his body the sackcloth with which he is encased, places that in naturally fitting parts with the bones, and taking from him also his sword puts that on the bed of leaves on the left side of the remains of mortality.

Next he throws on more dry wood, leaves and thatch, and having quite completed this part of his task, he, by some skilful method, noiselessly drives his pointed rod into a flame and sets the heap he has made on fire.

A sandal from the right foot of Simeon is finally made to burn until it is well scorched, is extinguished when half burnt away, and is laid a few yards in front of the blazing pyre, which they quickly leave behind them, to pursue a course westward but bearing a little to the north.

The fire, extending from the bed of leaves and wood and thatch to the chief hut, is carried to the other huts, and sets the whole of the ruined encampment into a magnificent blaze, visible for miles around.

The device is none too speedily executed; for the fugitives have but just sufficient time to reach a little wood, in which they lie concealed from the light shed by the fire, ere the Roman cavalry who left the encampment at the close of the revelry are at hand. The clatter of the hoofs of their horses is heard distinctly, as they are making for the fire.

The fugitives have not been seen by the pursuers, for the attention of every soldier has been fixed on the burning village.

But we, who have better eyes, are privileged to see an earlier messenger, on foot, who has witnessed every movement, every device, and who lies on the ground between the pursued and the burning village concealed perfectly himself and yet discerning all that transpires.

He is light of heart, for he has learned what none but one must know. His divine mistress, who has cast out from him the evil one, who has given him life, honour, duty, she alone must know. It is his first service for her.

The troops approach and gallop round the fire; first at a distance from it, for their horses, unaccustomed to so strange a sight, must be taught, gently, to draw near. In time they form a cordon around, from which not even a fox could escape without notice.

For indeed a fox, leaving her litter that she may survey the chances of escape, is perceived, is hooted back to the lair of her loves, and dies with them.

The ring of soldiery completed, the leader of the party with some of lesser degree dismount, and leaving their horses in charge of their men approach towards the chief entrance of the burning place. They pick up something that arrests their keen attention. They examine it together with nodding mystery.

A half-burnt sandal : the very sandal the Jew wore in the arena.

He ran until the fire caught his foot and then he fell. They will now find his remains. The fire is becoming much subdued. They lash together two javelins, and rake the fire at the entrance until they spread out what is left of the bed which Leon had constructed. They strike some solid thing and pull it out. It is a skull, black and burned into holes, but a skull. They strike more solid things, bones! bones! bones! They strike something that sounds on the iron head of the javelin like iron itself. Iron strikes iron. They drag out by the hook attached to the javelin that which is struck : it is a short sword, red-hot. Let it cool in the open air, until some one can touch it.

They are so impatient they would almost run the risk of burning their fingers in order to examine it. At last the captain of the troop ventures to lift it. They light him with a torch brought from the fire.

It is unquestionably the sword of the Jew Simeon. One of them knows it, for he has held it often in his hand, and it has the peculiarity that its handle is made of ebony. A portion of this handle is undestroyed and is ebony.

What can be clearer?

One thing more completes the find. The soldier with the javelin has dragged out a piece of sackcloth which is rotten with the fire and yet not consumed. It is a part of the sackcloth steeped in bitumen in which Simeon was enveloped before he ran as the living torch for the amusement of the people.

The chain of evidence is perfect. The living torch ran blindly into the plain until he accidentally caught sight of what, in the gloom, seemed to him a native village, where he might find succour. Before he reached the entrance the fire burned off his sandal, and so injured his foot that he fell at the gate of the place, fell there a blazing heap, and setting fire to the nest of desolation perished with it.

To-morrow, by daylight, more remains may be found; there is sufficient evidence for this time. They may return to the camp. They fix the skull on the head of the javelin that has been in the fire. They tie the long bones round the shaft of it. They tie together the short sword, the sandal and the sackcloth, and give over all these relics to a centurion for safe keeping.

The trumpet gives the note to resume marching order, and the order is obeyed like a natural law. The officers remount; the chief and his staff drop into their places in the rear, and gaily discussing the details of their expedition follow their men back into the encampment, just as the first light of day is exposing the departed glories of the night of revelry.

The pursuit over, the fugitives, resting awhile, prepare to continue their journey. Simeon is girt with new sandals, taken by the careful Leon from his never-failing wallet, which yields also food of a kind Simeon has never tasted before, and which gives him new strength. Water they find in a rivulet they have to cross, and full of energy they travel on. Leon leads, with the hand of Erine in his, and Simeon travels by their side.

With the first appearance of the glorious sun Leon and his child offer up their devotions to the mighty Power who refills the world with life.

Simeon also in his way adores the God of his fathers.

As Leon and Erinc return to him in the light of the sun, which now, just above the horizon, forms a background to their forms, they seem to him still like two celestial beings. His sight is dazed, and he would fall on his face before them did they not each take his hands, Leon his right, Erinc his left hand, and lift him from the ground.

Surely, he thinks, they have come out of the sun and their voices are voices of angels.

They are indeed sent for his deliverance.

They wander on in the early dawn until they reach a deep and long valley which, filled with mist painted by the rays of the sun, looks to them as a sea of molten gold. Out of this sea the tops of the trees stand like ships on the ocean to which the moving mist gives the appearance of motion. The trees bend in graceful action to the wind, and appear to sail along in a current swift and glorious.

To Simeon and Erinc the idea that they have reached the shores of a golden ocean is too delightful to be repressed. They run along the ridge of the hill on which they are placed.

They take each other's hand like children as they are, and return to Leon, their faces bright as the scene around them.

'Oh, father mine!' cries Erine, 'is this the sea where our faithful crew will meet us? surely it will carry us to realms of heaven.'

'Or to the city of Zion,' exclaimed Simeon, 'whence my people came whom I am to restore.'

'Sit down, my children, sit down and let me tell you the truth. This sea is a mirage, the sun god on high playing with the sons of men. See you not that the sea sinks, that yon sailing object, as it seems to us, moves more slowly, grows taller, becomes what it is, a tree. The sea sinks, no, the vapour rises and the winds clear it away. The bed of the sea becomes a valley, a valley full of trees, and meadows, and flowers and sward.

'Now there is no more sea.'

And while he speaks what was a golden ocean a few minutes before, full of life and motion, is a quiet valley filled with light alone.

For a moment the hearts of the young people are cast down, but soon their longing vision is cheered with a new and equally beautiful sight. The valley seems to expand, to open at its farther extremity, and to allow mountains far away to show their blue crests like pinnacles piercing the skies from which their colours are derived.

Soon also in the distance they catch sight of another new object, a river which beyond the gorge of the valley, on its western side, winds its way like a vein of pure silver let into the earth. Upon this streak of silver Leon, by some process unknown to Simeon, takes his observations. With steady and precise care he measures the intervening space; from a dial with a moving hand, he determines the direction in which he wishes to move; and, fully prepared for the journey he has in view, he once more leads them on.

It is a day of rapture, a day in which by that youth and maiden, a life of life is lived.

The noble Leon leads them towards some place he has definitely in view: but gentle Erine Leoline, lioness with a woman's heart, whither leadest thou the son of destiny?

They traverse the ridge of the valley towards the west, and in a short time approach a forest, above which on one side is a rising ground overlooking the forest itself and all around it.

Ascending this height Leon proceeds to wield another power. By the movement of a bright metallic plate he casts a sign or beacon towards the distant river, but now broader and better defined. In return there falls upon himself flashes of light like rays of the sun, which communicate by some hidden language a reply to what he has asked to know.

At length to Erine, who stands by accustomed to watch the proceeding and prepared for a message, he tells what he has learned.

' Our faithful servants and the caravel lie safely concealed at the point where yon silver stream bends to the north-west. We are four leagues away, and between us and them in a straight line there are two Roman encampments. We must take to the woods, and by a two days' circuit we shall reach our destination unperceived. I have signalled that in two sunsets we shall be with them, and they are content.'

Descending from their height they enter by a ravine into a splendid forest, which they traverse with a new pleasure. Now they wander through labyrinths of darkness; then they enter into a glade in which a natural temple is produced before them. They cross it reverently, in a gloom almost as profound as night itself; but Leon has a light to help them and bids them not to fear. He goes before, and Simeon and Erine, hand in hand, follow, and are afraid.

Afraid, not of the gloom of the glade but of the coming time when their hands, so firmly and innocently clasped, must part sweet company.

They listen to a sound, the soft tinkling of a bell or a chime. They step forward more carefully and softly as through the trees the rays of light are glinting faintly. The light increases in fulness, and suddenly they enter a natural citadel as it seems to them, a citadel cut out of the midst of the forest, but, except for the musical sounds, quiet as a sepulchre.

Into this place of dazzling splendour the sun beams with all his might; before them, at a distance of some hundred feet, is a mountain of stone like a mound, with a fountain at its top and a pool surrounding it at its base. From the fountain water falls in riplets into the pool below, and the resonant pile gives out the sound like a chime of melodious bells. They ascend a rock on the side of this natural tower, and see, in full, the beauty of the spot. Leon explains that the central mound of stone from which the water runs over was once the mouth of a volcano, by which all this place was originally cleft. The mouth of the crater has long been closed at its lower part, and a spring of water derived from the higher surrounding rocks has found its way by a subterranean channel into the open basin, whence, at times, the water flows over into the little moat below, from which it finds a passage into the earth again. That little accident keeps, he says, this otherwise dead spot of earth alive. The water falls over, casting up spray, the sun converts the spray into vapour, the vapour descends in mist and dew when the sun goes to rest, and so seeds and trees and mosses and shrubs find their nourishment and thrive luxuriantly.

The foxgloves specially, with their exquisite forms and colours and drooping bells, please the young pair.

'Admire but touch not, my children; in

that plant lies concealed what would kill all
your admiration. The learned Greeks have
called it the plant which kills the heart.'

Around this volcanic pit or basin of rocks
shrubs, ferns, and trees grow, leaving between
them and the central mound a walk of white
smooth stone, like marble, from which running
into the side of the rocks are caves of great
depth and varied shape. Birds nestle and
sing in the shrubs, and now and then a startled
rabbit rushes forth, and sitting on the top
of a rock looks round in wonder that his
quiet home should be molested. But there
is no sign of any wild or dangerous animal.

They enter a cave which faces the sun in
his glory, breaking before them the shrubs and
briars which obstruct the entrance.

The cave is cut and arched as if it had
been the work of the most skilled architect.
It is grooved within into a kind of horizontal
spiral, from which chambers jut out at graceful angles. The first of these chambers and
the largest is so near the chief entrance it is
lighted to the highest point of a roof which
seems to be made up of the bodies of animals
in petrified forms, extant and motionless for

ages. Its floor is of the same white veined stone as that of the pathway outside. In the convulsion of nature which made all the place that floor and path were once a molten lime which cooled into level solidity and now lies frozen eternally. With these natural wonders Leon is transported, but, seeing how wearied his companions are, he prepares for their refreshment and repose. What he does Simeon watches with liveliest interest, but no longer with wonder. His mind is at ease. This man, this girl, are his ministering angels. If they turn the very stones into bread it will be no marvel to him now; the thing would be done for him in pursuance of the decrees which have sent him forth.

Stones are not turned into bread, but food is soon prepared. They traverse the paths of the rocks, and from certain of the plants which Leon points out they pluck the fruit. They gather from the earth some sweet smelling herbs which he recognises as edible; they turn a large hollow shell like a piece of rock into a pitcher which they fill with water from the falling streamlets in the central pile; and, so enriched, they return to the cave, where Erine soon lays out the choicest repast the enthusiastic Simeon has, he thinks, ever seen; a repast to which Leon, from his matchless wallet, adds cakes for food, and silver cups for holding the water that quenches their thirst.

On the floor of the cave Simeon and his leader make seats out of the loose stones, covering the seats with the mosses which grow so luxuriantly amongst the rocks around. And thus prepared they break their long fast.

They form a mystical group. In each there is of its kind a surpassing beauty. Erine, sitting a little raised between the two men, is peerless. Never before has Simeon seen such loveliness; eyes, pure and blue as the sky, into which the rapt observer sinks as into an azure sea; a face fair of the fairest, and faultless in its outline; lips and mouth, and expression of gentlest holiest love; and all set in a framework of golden hair which, falling like an avalanche over shoulders of ivory, is, in its very disorder, natural and comely. Her dress of white, lightly open at the throat and bosom, clothes her from the shoulders to the feet, and her green scarf, passed under her avalanche of golden tresses, covers also her shoulders, and falling richly and loosely over her knees makes her look like a plant of heaven rising from the earth in all its youth, its gracefulness and strength.

Her companions on either side of her are little less remarkable than herself. She sits between the pillars of wisdom and strength.

Simeon is buoyant in spite of all he has gone through. He wears still the dress in which he appeared in the arena, except that his feet are clad in the new and strong sandals which his host has lent to him, and his head is covered with a leathern cap or berretta, the most elegant head-dress ever worn by the male part of mankind. It is a dress alto-gether—excepting for the new sandals—which he has designed for his sword and athletic practice, but it suits him as gracefully for peace as for combat.

His face is the face of Spain and of Judah; a perfect mould of symmetrical cast. The forehead rather narrow and retreating, with dark hair above; the eyebrows arched, the eyes deep hazel, full, luminous, and wonder-ing; the nose is aquiline, the nostrils slightly

expanded ; the lips and cheeks well filled,
and firm set with command of the most
winning smile ; the chin just prominent with
a rather deep but well-formed cleft betwixt
it and the lower lip ; the complexion a pale
olive ; the expression serene to the maximum
of serenity. The limbs are models of strength
and freedom ; and the whole frame a living
engine of trained athletic skill.

Leon looking at the youth, from time to
time, sums him up slowly and calmly as a
new artistic study in the domain of life, while
Simeon in turn watches, with keenest observation, the man whose voice he has heard, whose
hand he has clasped, whose outline he has
seen, and whose protection he has experienced,
but whose face and manner are new to him in
the light of day.

The protector is indeed not one for Simeon
merely to see and therewith be content. He
is a man who, once spoken with, is at once
recognised as remarkable above other men.
His wide and accurate knowledge and his art
of research into hidden things account, in a
large degree, for this fact ; but his appearance
adds to the effect. Simeon instinctively recog-

nises both influences. He sees a man much
older, but as strong, he believes, as himself, a
man really not youthful to the eye yet bearing no trace of age. Like the child he owns,
the man is of fair complexion, of a sanguine
tint which tells both of activity and power.
By one of those happy racial admixtures
which make up the varieties of the flowering
garden of humanity, his hair is an iron grey,
while his eyes are of the same deep blue as
those of his child, and equally absorptive.
His head is a dome of perfect symmetry and
balance; the eyebrows are lengthened with
the large capacious brow; the expression of
countenance is that of dignity, knowledge,
and wisdom. He is also strong of body and
graceful, but deliberate of movement; his
speech is winning, hopeful and trustful. Above
all, there is in his voice the charm that makes
him a charmer of men; it is a voice of music
rich in cadences, and so sweet to hear that
when it ceases the listeners wait as if something
they still wished to hear had yet to come.
But for this delicious melody of speech it might
be felt that from his richness of knowledge
he spoke too frequently and too long. A

harsh voice would make him a pain ; a hesitant
speech would make him a bore, from whom all
would flee ; but the sweetness of his tune and
the firmness of his tone, varied with natural
art to suit the subject on which he descants,
removes all weariness of mind or fear of
failure, and holds every one captive who comes
under its fascinating spell.

The three form a picture it is hard to
leave. Suffice it to record at this moment
that they converse with facility in the Latin
tongue, and that their discourse is as cheerful
as it is fluent and friendly ; after which they
take their morning rest.

Into one of the side recesses of the inner
cave already described, Leon out of soft plants
and branches of trees and heaps of mosses and
flowers, makes a bed for his beloved child. He
carries her, drooping with sleep, in his arms as
when she was a motherless infant to whom all
his life was to be devoted, and lays her, unre-
sisting, on the improvised couch. He smooths
her tresses, smooths the folds of her dress,
casts over her his own mantle, and receiving
from her lips the half-conscious filial kiss
which is ever the last act of her wakeful day,
he watches over her innocent face, innocent

and lovely as the choicest flowers near to her, till she sleeps like them. He sees her eyelids fall, he hears her breathing almost mute, he returns her kiss without response from her, and knowing now that she has sunken into the oblivion that restores to life, he softly and noiselessly steals from her side.

He starts, as he regains the outer court of the cave, to find that his other companion, who but a minute or two ago was so full of vigorous life and action, now lies in equally death-like oblivion. In a moment, in the twinkling of an eye, sleep has entrapped the valiant youth whom he has saved. On the rocky mound on which he sits Simeon has fallen back into a kind of chair or couch of rock, in an attitude so peaceful he seems a sculptured figure in the wall of the cave, left by a hand divine in art. He has unconsciously fallen in the line of beauty, and sleep has seated him firm as the stones on which he reposes. So deep is the oblivion that Leon, unable to detect movements of his chest, holds over his nostrils a polished plate to see if moisture from the breath of life can be caught upon it.

Satisfied that the sleep which revivifies

is the sleep alone that suspends the life of his *protégé*, he gently moves back the luxuriant curls from off the handsome face, and with the skill of the learned student of physiognomy reads the character of the sleeper.

It is a complicated reading. Innocence blends with courage, courage with a resolution scarcely mortal, defying men, time, and death.

The dress of the sleeper, open at the bosom, exposes a small square of woven substance suspended by a band of silk loosely tied round the neck; on this the eye of Leon falls.

It is a trifling thing this little square of woven substance, and yet it has the instant effect of filling the eyes of him who now surveys it with a flood of tears. It bears in curious characters a date; it bears the face of a beautiful woman; a date, a face, that marks in lines of grief the two most appalling events of his, the observer's, career. That face is like the face of his dead wife ; that date is the date of the day when she, dying, gave birth to a boy who never lived.

Did this sleeping youth come into the world alive, on the day when his son, his only son, came into the world dead ?

With gentle hand he lifts the woven square,
to turn it over and see the other side.   As the
relic leaves the breast of the sleeper, he starts
from head to foot, as if his soul were being
torn from him; his face grows deathly, his
hands clench.   But as the relic overcast falls
back on the surface of his body, he also falls
back, and once again sleeps.

A thrill of wonder, enthusiasm, and admiration passes now through Leon the philosopher.

The obverse of the woven square is
marked with symbols which he can read.

'The son of an illustrious King before
whom the stars fled, and of Palestrina of the
Temple, sent to deliver his people from bondage
and tribulation.'

The signs indicating these words are
enclosed in an embroidered square repre-
senting the earth.   On the eastern side of this
square is the design of a youth with a star
on his forehead, bearing aloft a torch of fire.
At the upper part of the square is the sun in
his meridian glory ; at the western side another

youth is sitting, with his head downcast and his torch extinguished in the earth. They are symbols of one who is to rise in brightness, attain meridian glory, sink into gloom, and leave the world still in its darkness, pain, and sorrow.

No, not leave it so hopeless ; for see at the foot of the square there is the moon as a cradle borne by the constellation Leo of the stars, and in that cradle the youth reclines. The light of the moon and stars is faintly reflected by the star still on his brow.

He is not dead ! He is being carried away to new glories. He will arise again, and in some newer and holier form reanimate the world that mourns his absent face.

The countenance of Leon the scholar is transformed with wonder. In this cave he has found, as the prophetic legend declares shall be found, the child of the sun in human form, to redeem mankind. The incarnate Mithras is here. The lion and the star of that country in the East from which his own fathers were exiled by the barbarians of the mountains have re-united. He, Leon of the west, has met the star of the east. His dead son lives again, as his dead wife lives again in the angelic girl sleeping in that other cave.

The learned books of his people, in which he is the most learned, have foretold the whole. He must read the symbols anew.

There is no error in the reading. In this savage Britain, land of savages and of Romans who are little better, this youth, a few hours agone a running torch, running to please a murderous crew, is now revealed to him as a torch for lighting humanity to its farthest stretch of glory. A priestess must have formed those symbols, written them in a Holy Temple as ascending, in spirit, through the sacred dome of light, she descended in body to the silent palaces of the dead!

Taking care to return the woven tablet without ever letting it lose its touch with the body of the sleeper, Leon restores the tablet as he had originally found it.

By this time the light of the sun fills each part of the cave, leaving no shadow, but giving to the stalactite pendants on the roof a hundred points of incandescence which cast a glow upon the youth, suggesting to the entranced philosopher a more than earthly beauty, over

which he sits down to reflect and wonder.
Gradually the music of the falling water
absorbs his senses, and from thinking of the
symbols he has read he lapses into a vague
counting of the musical drops of the cascades.
The sounds become metrical, and chime to him
inconsequent words, of which the following
poor translation may convey an idea :—

Drop! drop! drop!
Myriads of drops in an hour
Drop! drop! drop!
Myriads of drops in a shower.

Splash! splash! splash!
Rise up in bubbles and fly;
Splash! splash! splash!
Sink into oceans and die.

And so for a time we will leave this mystic
three under the safe protection of Him who is
their strength and their shield.

END OF THE FIRST VOLUME.

PRINTED BY
SPOTTISWOODE AND CO., NEW-STREET SQUARE
LONDON

www.ingramcontent.com/pod-product-compliance
Lightning Source LLC
Chambersburg PA
CBHW020855020726
47497CB00005B/1418